T0168640

The American Poetry Recovery Series

Series Editor
Cary Nelson

Board of Advisors

Daniel Aaron

Houston A. Baker, Jr.

Carolyn Forché

Karen Ford

Reginald Gibbons

Paul Lauter

Philip Levine

Alan Wald

Books in The American Poetry Recovery Series

Collected Poems
Edwin Rolfe; edited by Cary Nelson and Jefferson Hendricks

Trees Became Torches: Selected Poems
Edwin Rolfe; edited by Cary Nelson and Jefferson Hendricks

Trees Became Torches

EDWIN ROLFE

TREES BECAME TORCHES

Selected Poems

EDITED BY

Cary Nelson & Jefferson Hendricks

INTRODUCTION AND NOTES

BY CARY NELSON

UNIVERSITY OF ILLINOIS PRESS

Urbana and Chicago

Digitally reprinted from the first paperback printing

Publication of this book was supported by a grant from
the National Endowment for the Arts.

© 1995 by the Board of Trustees of the University of Illinois
Manufactured in the United States of America
P 5 4 3 2 1

This book is printed on acid-free paper.

Library of Congress Cataloging-in-Publication Data

Rolfe, Edwin, 1909–1954.
   [Poems. Selections]
   Trees became torches : selected poems / Edwin Rolfe ; edited by
Cary Nelson and Jefferson Hendricks ; introduction and notes
by Cary Nelson.
     p. cm. — (American poetry recovery series)
   ISBN 0-252-06417-8 (pbk. : alk. paper)
   I. Nelson, Cary. II. Hendricks, Jefferson, 1953-   . III. Title.
IV. Series.
PS3535.0476A6   1995
811'.52—dc20
                                         94-6722
                                          CIP

CONTENTS

CONTENTS

CONTENTS

LYRIC POLITICS:
THE POETRY OF EDWIN ROLFE

Cary Nelson

Sometimes I wake at night
out of completest sleep
and see their remembered faces
luminous in the dark.
Ghostly as tracer-bullets
their smiles, their hesitant speech,
their eloquent hands in gesture
and their smiles belying fear:
Antonio, Catalan,
eighteen years old . . . Hilario, filling
his lungs with power and purpose.

If there's any place in the world where I could be dropped
from an airplane, alone, blind-folded, in pitch darkness,
and yet know from the very smell and feel and slope of the
earth exactly where I was—that would be the hills and
valley just east of the Ebro, in Spain.

These fragments come from notebooks that Edwin Rolfe (1909–54)—poet, journalist, and veteran of the Spanish Civil War—kept during the late 1940s and early 1950s.[1] The first recalls some of the young Spanish soldiers who filled out the depleted ranks of a group of mostly American volunteers—the Lincoln Battalion—in the spring of 1938; the second recalls the last great campaign that Rolfe and the other Lincolns fought when they crossed the Ebro River that summer. It was on the hills and in the valleys east of the Ebro, a day's travel southwest from Barcelona, that Rolfe and other members of the International Brigades trained in during the spring and summer of 1938. And it was just east of the river that they assembled their forces before crossing to engage Franco's troops that July. Although he completed a number of poems about Spain both while he was there from 1937 to 1938 and in the decade that followed his return to the United States in 1939, Rolfe's body of work includes as well a number of fragments like these that suggest a continuing (and significantly less finished) dialogue with himself and his culture about the meaning of this most passionate of all 1930s commitments.

Spain was the focus of the second of the three books of poems Rolfe gathered for publication, *First Love and Other Poems* (1951). The first was *To My Contemporaries* (1936); the third was *Permit Me Refuge* (1955), assembled and introduced by Thomas McGrath from a manuscript Rolfe was working on at the time of his death. In addition to being at the center of his career, Spain was also for him, as for so many of those who fought there, an experience that became in some ways the fulcrum of his life. The experience in Spain provided him with a way of thinking about much that was admirable in the revolutionary Left of the twenties and thirties as well as a contrast to the dark decade and more of national repression that followed World War II.

We open Rolfe's *Selected Poems* with his Spanish poems, then, in order to acknowledge what was for Rolfe the most fulfilling political moment of his life. The book's title, *Trees Became Torches,* is taken from "City of Anguish," a poem about the bombing of Madrid that Rolfe wrote when he was living there in the fall of 1937. We close the book, on the other hand, with some of Rolfe's final poems and with his most challenging legacy to his American readers—his poems taking up the long postwar inquisition that culminated in the period that has come to be called the McCarthy era. In reading the poems that open *Trees Became Torches* we encounter Rolfe's most overtly lyrical work. It is there that readers who feel hailed by Rolfe's language and his passion can discover part of what is most distinctive about his poetry—that in Rolfe's work the lyrical voice becomes a politically positioned subject. At the end of *Trees Became Torches* we can discover that American poets of the late 1940s and early 1950s did not only write about family life and classical myth; the poems of "Summons to the Inquisition" help recover poetry's more critical role in the culture of paranoia, terror, and conformity that reigned in the postwar years. Indeed, if we are to resist repression in the future, we need to know its role in our own history.

After his death, Rolfe's comrades in Spain came to think of him as their poet laureate. He is certainly the American poet who did the most sustained work about the Spanish Civil War; he may well also be the poet who did the most sustained work about McCarthyism. McGrath's foreword to *Permit Me Refuge* is worth quoting in its entirety, because it marks the stages of this career and the way one of Rolfe's close friends and contemporaries regarded it:

> In a time like ours all true poems have to be laments or manifestoes. There have been other such times; but perhaps it is only in ours that the poem has to be both things at once.
> Edwin Rolfe grew up in the city, became a radical, was a maker of manifestoes. Later, although he loved the variety of urban life, toward the last he

made some poems about its ugliness, its cruelty, the terrible anonymity of its people.

He was not just a writer: he fought for his belief in the Spanish war against Franco and fascism, against real bullet-shooting guns that could kill. He believed that the word must become flesh, that saying and doing must become one.

I think it is one of the finest things about Rolfe that after initial popular successes he moved on to explore more difficult country. This last group of poems shows us bench-marks of that long survey.

I want to bear down on this, because it is an almost impossible thing to overhaul a style, a method of making, after having had some measure of success in it. Yet he refused to repeat the easy successes of an earlier time and fought stubbornly for the way to name the new thing that a degenerate age had created. This brought a new wryness and toughness into some of his poems. He had crossed the cold summit, the height-of-land, had found the best way for his speech.

These poems are the first things in the beginning of his best period. In that sense they are first poems rather than last, though it would be hard to surpass such earlier things as his "Definition," "Elegy for Our Dead," or "First Love."

Rolfe had a gentleness that was shocking. Just the same, there was a lot of iron in him. He was capable of fury and rage. But no malice. He was very good with young writers, although they, lacking a knowledge of the ground of his experiences, usually found it easier to love than to understand him.

He was a *serious* poet—that is to say, he did not believe that one could create a whole corpus of work out of little moral or mock-moral allegories concerning birds and animals, or out of the eccentric learning of pedantic uncles. He was always smelling the real sweat of the terrible Now, the terrible Always. Probably all really good poems have that smell.

So, at the last, you could say that he suffered and he acted. The writing was more than the suffering because he was a revolutionary and, simultaneously, a poet. How hard this is to be, true poets and revolutionaries may know. At the end he was trying to write that not-quite-yet-written poem which is both lament and triumph. A hard work, and as good a signature as any.

To write at the intersection of lament and triumph was, for Rolfe, to write as a witness to history. He began to focus on the fragility and necessity of historical memory—on its key place in maintaining an informed and viable politics— almost immediately upon returning from Spain in 1939. At the largest narrative level, the Spanish Civil War was the historical event that set the tone for the whole subsequent struggle between democracy and fascism. It was also a unique moment when men and women across the world came together to give their lives for a cause in which they believed. Despite the massive loss of life typical of modern war and despite the special anguish of a civil conflict, the effort to aid the elected Spanish government in its struggle against fascism represented a triumph of internationalism, whether in support of democratic socialism, the ideals of communism, or the common interests of the working classes. It was in part the selflessness of that commitment that was recognized when the International Brigades held their farewell march through Barcelona on October 29, 1938. Unique in history, it was a parade to honor brigades that were part of what many realized would likely soon become a defeated army. As Rolfe would write nine years later in an unfinished poem, "Even the day of defeat / Exalted us." As part of the parade—in what must seem an improbable gesture by our contemporary political and poetic standards—printed poems commemorating the occasion were passed among the crowd.

Rolfe was there, and he saved some of those poem cards and brought them back to the United States. It was a lesson about what role poetry might play in alerting readers to the crucial matters of their day. Poetry was to be at once a call to witness—a sign of where it mattered to stand and an example of the voice one might assume in standing there—and the essence of the historical record, its most succinct and telling form of testimony. In a few months Rolfe returned to his own country, where those who stood with Spain were scandalized as "premature antifascists." In less than a decade, many began losing their jobs in the massive postwar purge of the Left. As Rolfe wrote in an unpublished stanza he revised repeatedly, to remember Spain in those days was to stand against the dominant culture and against the national madness:

> Let the callous and secure, who have so much to lose,
> Forget Spain's passion and agony. Memory's an encumbrance,
> Embarrassing, even dangerous at times. For myself I
>   choose—
> Because to forget is to betray—the pain of remembrance.

The cost of forgetting would be paid both in our collective public life—in a curtailed knowledge of political possibilities, resources, and consequences—and in each one of us. Rolfe describes some of the individual cost in another unfinished postwar fragment:

> This is the age of the made-over man
> Name changed, perhaps,
> whose life is cut in half as by a knife

(and, like the worm, each half goes on living)
who must, if he is clever and cautious, forget
the first and passionate years in favor of
his made-over self, which must suppress
all memory; his made-over self
which is cunning at last, and uninvolved,
and slyly garbed in protective colored-suit
which he dare not divest himself of, even for a minute,
not even for sleep, if he wants to feel safe.
Not even for sleeping, lest his true history
rise in his dream to confront him.

Rolfe's career began with the "first and passionate" social and political commitments commemorated in this fragment. They are evident here not only in the section "Work and Revolution" but throughout the book. The strong political statements in Rolfe's poems came fairly naturally to him; although they reflect his own experiences and political activities, they also flow partly from his family background.[2] His father was a socialist and an official of a union local in New York. His mother was active in the birth control movement, pitched in during the famous 1913 silk workers' strike in Paterson, New Jersey, and later joined the Communist party. At the flat on Coney Island in New York where they lived for much of Rolfe's childhood, they let rooms to other people to help cover the rent; one such tenant was a red-headed Wobbly from the West—a member of our most irreverent, disruptive, and populist union, the Industrial Workers of the World—who used to give Rolfe and his younger brother, Bern, rides on his motorcycle and tell them stories of IWW organizing. Rolfe himself joined the Young Communist League in 1925, when he was fifteen.[3] When he published his first poem in the *Daily Worker* in 1927, "The Ballad of the Subway Digger," it was a newspaper he already knew well at home.

Rolfe was born Solomon Fishman; his parents Nathan and Bertha emigrated from Jewish communities in Russia early in the century and met in Philadelphia, where they lived for the first few years of Rolfe's life. He began using pen names in high school, used the name "Edwin Rolfe" on some publications in the late 1920s, and by the early 1930s had effectively become Edwin Rolfe. Changing his name was a gesture that signaled at once his chosen identity as a writer and his conscious decision to commit himself to political activism.

After working intermittently in the already selectively depressed New York economy of the late 1920s, Rolfe wanted relief from the city and a chance to read and write in a less interrupted way. He was also ready to break with the Communist party, some of whose functionaries neither then nor later did he find sympathetic figures. Left politics, moreover, had been frequently disputatious during the 1920s; indeed, in one such dispute his parents had aligned themselves with different groups, and thus the political conflicts of the period also played themselves out in Rolfe's family.[4] In the fall of 1929 he quit the YCL and left New York to enroll in the Experimental College at the University of Wisconsin at Madison. As his advisors noted, he retained strong loyalties to the working classes,[5] but for most of the next year he avoided politics and instead read widely and wrote relatively nonpolitical poems, including three written in 1929 or 1930 and published in *Pagany* in 1932. As the depression deepened, however, he was drawn to politics again and left Wisconsin in the middle of his second year there.

Rolfe rejoined the YCL in New York and, after a variety of temporary jobs, began working full time at the *Daily Worker*. This was the period when the Party was beginning to shift toward becoming part of a mass movement. In the midst of massive unemployment, vast dislocation, and widespread hunger—and little faith that capitalism would recover—many here and in Europe were radicalized. For a time revolutionary social and political change seemed possible. Dozens of radical journals sprang up, not only in large cities but also in small towns and rural communities across the country. Radical theater drew audiences from all classes. Political art appeared in public places. Despite considerable suffering, the midthirties were thus a heady time on the Left. Much of the poetry of the period combines sharp social critique with a sense of revolutionary expectation. More than simply reflecting the times, however, the "proletarian" poetry of revolution sought to define a new politics, to suggest subject positions within it, and to help bring about the changes it evoked.[6] Far from a solitary romantic vocation, thirties political poetry is a form of collaborative rhetorical action, as poets respond to one another by ringing changes on similar revolutionary themes and metaphors.

"Asbestos," published in the *Daily Worker* in 1928, anticipates the sympathies he would refine and indicates what he was capable of even at an early age; a stunning, if gruesome, conceit transforms a worker's body into his deathbed:

> John's deathbed is a curious affair:
> the posts are made of bone, the spring of nerves,
> the mattress bleeding flesh. Infinite air,
> compressed from dizzy altitudes, now serves

his skullface as a pillow. Overhead
a vulture leers in solemn mockery,
knowing what John had never known: that dead
workers are dead before they cease to be.

The exploitation of workers, we learn, literally impresses itself on their bodies. Those bodies are the fulcrum, the point of application, of all the power relations in which their lives are embedded. Yet the poem's very fluency, its metaphorical bravado, embeds political resistance within social tragedy. Rolfe was only nineteen when he wrote the poem, but he had learned a lesson that would help carry him through the rest of his career. It was first of all a lesson about class relations and about how they play themselves out in the industrial workplace. But it was also a lesson about how political poetry can take up traditional lyric forms—here the rhymed quatrains of the ballad stanza—and give them fresh social meaning. Both the *abab* rhyme scheme and the character's generic name (John is a common name in ballads and folk poems) might lead us to expect a conventional folk tale, but the power of the central conceit and the recurrent enjambments disturb the potential for predictability. The partial echo of the ballad form, then, creates a context that the poem's content violates, though the generic form also reminds us that the poem's unique metaphor points to social relations that are anything but unique. For the poem demonstrates that the popular imagination of the time must encompass the culture's exploitation of the ordinary worker; John *is* the everyman of the twenties and thirties industrial state.

Rolfe was writing such poems, it is important to realize, in 1927 and 1928, months before the stock market crash in 1929 and years before the worst of the depression. He had grown up on the Left, and among his strongest influences as a young man were two notable friends from the older generation of the Left of the twenties, Joseph Freeman and Mike Gold. He took a writing class from Gold and was among the young people who often gathered at Freeman's house for conversation. Gold later wrote the introduction to *We Gather Strength* (1933), a collection of poems by Herman Spector, Joseph Kalar, Rolfe, and Sol Funaroff. Rolfe also knew other people associated with *The Masses* and *The Liberator;* Floyd Dell, for example, wrote Rolfe a recommendation for college. In any case, Rolfe was among those whose evolving political sensibilities prepared him to understand the depression in a particular way and to act on that understanding. He entered the thirties with deep sympathies for working people; by the time the collapse of the economy seemed irreversible, Rolfe was thoroughly devoted to international socialism as the only real alternative to continuing economic misery, destructive nationalist rivalries, and the basic racism of American culture. Lest we think such convictions quixotic, we might, for example, remember that in 1932 some fifty-three writers and artists—including John Dos Passos, Langston Hughes, and Edmund Wilson—signed the pamphlet *Culture and Crisis* that urged people to support the Communist party in that year's presidential election.

Rolfe's own commitments began earlier and continued longer, but the special force and coherence of the poems written before he left for Spain in 1937 grew out of the historical context of the Great Depression. "They who work here know no other things," he wrote earlier, "only heat and smoke and fumes of baking bricks." Now he offers a vision of "America today: its / fields plowed under . . . its wide / avenues blistered by sun and poison gas." "They who have reaped your harvest," he warns, merely "offer you the stalks." "This is the season when rents go up: / men die, and their dying is casual"; "their blood is dust now borne into the air"; "you see the dead face peering from your shoes; / the eggs at Thompson's are the dead man's eyes":

> This is the sixth winter:
> this is the season of death
> when lungs contract and the breath of homeless men
> freezes on restaurant window panes. . . .
>
> The forest falls, the stream runs dry,
> the tree rots visibly to the ground;
> nothing remains but sixteen black
> bodies against a blood-red sky.

Only revolutionary change will suffice, and the responsibility of the revolutionary poet is to combine conviction with the intricacies of technique. In the first stanza above we read the first two exclamatory lines—"This is the sixth winter: / this is the season of death"—each in a single breath—for the lines are perfectly cadenced and pointedly terse. Rolfe achieves this effect with the internal assonance of the repeated short *i*'s, the sibilance of the alliterated *s*'s, the initial "this is," and the controlled dactyls. But in the third line he lets his breath out; a medial caesura falls, the meter degrades, and we must draw breath as do the homeless men.

Technique, however, never overshadows Rolfe's subject matter, for his focus throughout his career was political and historical; he believed that we live in history and that it is within and to history that even the supposedly more transcendent arts speak. Yet Rolfe's poems are also in their own way strikingly personal. For history to him is never the object of a disinterested gaze but rather the substance of his daily life: the context of his memories, the ground of current struggle, and the basis—when hope is possible—of any actions aimed toward the future. His life, then, is intricately woven into these poems; indeed he based many poems on his and his friends' personal experiences. Sometimes the personal context is partly or wholly elided; when we could, we have supplied those contexts here or in the notes because we believe they make the poems richer and more complex, rather than restrict their meaning to "merely" autobiographical references. More specifically, they let us see some of what is at stake for Rolfe in transmuting personal experience into poems that are politically and historically useful. For Rolfe's poetry disavows the lyrical belief that anything personal can be wholly exceptional; both he and his friends lived extraordinary but in some ways representative lives. Whether struggling to find work in the depression, burying a dead comrade in Spain, or resisting the anticommunist madness of the postwar decades, Rolfe and the other people written into these poems acted in response to the times in which they lived. These poems are therefore not simply Rolfe's legacy but rather history's legacy to us. They are a testimony to what history gave to us, demanded of us, and took away from us in the decades in which Rolfe lived. And they urge us to reexamine our national past if we are to have any chance of acting responsibly and progressively in the present. To take up a position and act in relation to the cultural struggles history imposes on us is, finally, a major part of what it means to Rolfe to be alive.

It may help us to understand the historical weight of individual experience in Rolfe's work if we restore some of the biographical details the poems eliminate. A few such examples will also suggest a good deal about the relationship of personal experience to Rolfe's process of composition:

"Room with Revolutionists" is dedicated to "J.F." (Joseph Freeman) and in fact is based on a conversation between Freeman and the Mexican painter David Alfaro Siqueros. That much is confirmed both in Rolfe's letters to Freeman and in Freeman's own correspondence.[7] Rolfe describes Freeman as "brother, Communist, friend, / counsellor of my youth and manhood." The focus of the poem, however, is on the mix of similarity and difference in revolutionary commitments in Freeman's and Siqueros's respective cultures. One man is most known for his writing, the other for his painting. One works on behalf of the Mexican "poor who burrow / under the earth in field and mine," the other on behalf of American working people. But they are also bound together by a vision that "transcends all frontiers." It was possible then, in the midst of the 1930s, to grasp an international solidarity that overrode national differences. Knowing that Rolfe had specific people in mind helps us realize that he was reflecting on the political implications of actual practices, not on some unrealizable internationalist utopia. Yet the elimination of their identities from the poem also reinforces the idea that these and comparable roles can be filled by a variety of people. And the poem demonstrates that, even before Spain, Rolfe was drawn to the idea of an international revolutionary movement.

"Epitaph" is dedicated to Arnold Reid, who died on July 27, 1938, at Villalba de los Arcos in Spain. In fact, when Rolfe published the poem in *New Masses* in 1939 he called it "For Arnold Reid." What we know from the poem is that Reid was a friend of Rolfe's and that he was among the American volunteers who gave their lives in the Ebro campaign that summer. There is a great deal else about Reid and Rolfe's relationship with him, however, that the poem holds at a distance. Much of this is not "in" the poem at all, but it is arguably part of what Rolfe negotiated in order to write the poem. In putting all this material back into an active relationship with "Epitaph," I may be burdening its three stanzas with more than they can easily carry. But this exercise gives us a clear opportunity to establish some of what can be at stake in the complex negotiations between poetry, autobiography, and history, relations we have ignored for too long.

What we might not know without reading about the war itself is that Reid was a political commissar in Barcelona and did not have to leave and go into battle.[8] Like Rolfe, who left his post as editor of *Volunteer for Liberty*, the English-language magazine of the International Brigades, so that he could join his comrades in the field, Reid chose to leave Barcelona and put himself at risk. Rolfe was thus in a sense acknowledging that double commitment—first to go to Spain and then to take up active duty when there was an alternative readily available.

Rolfe actually met Reid nine years earlier, in 1929, when they were both students at the University of Wisconsin. At the time Reid was still Arnold Reisky, though he was already a committed Communist and was soon to change his name to make it easier to be a party organizer among people who were more comfortable with names that sounded conventionally American. Reisky was Rolfe's first good friend in college, and they often debated the virtues of political commitment. Rolfe had quit the Party and in May 1930 wrote to another friend that "Reisky has found me guilty of being a renegade from the Holy

Cause."[9] Standing over his grave—"we buried him / here where he fell"—some of this history no doubt comes back to him. It was certainly in his mind earlier in July when he talked with Reid about their Wisconsin days and again a few months later when he wrote "His Name Was Arnold Reid: An American on the Honor Roll of the Ebro's Dead," a prose piece published in the October 4, 1938, issue of *New Masses*. There he acknowledges that they were classmates at Wisconsin and talks briefly about their friendship.

"Epitaph" was written on July 30, 1938. Three days after Reid was killed, Rolfe returned to his battlefield grave to write an elegy on the spot where he died. Reid's blood, Rolfe imagines, will now nourish the vineyards and olive groves of the surrounding hills. Yet it will also run "deeper than grave was dug / ever," deep enough to feed those fields "no enemy's boots / can ever desecrate," fields sown in honor of Spain's democratic revolution and its devotion to equality for all people. These are not, therefore, for Rolfe the conventional fields of heaven, for he is not that sort of believer, but rather fields of historical memory and witness, fields traced by the camaraderie of shared commitment, the mutual recognition of historical understanding, and the record of things done. Those too are the fields of Spain—fields that for Rolfe represent the material history of an ideal—and thus they are fields no enemy can capture.

Perhaps Rolfe had in mind the 1937 antifascist portfolio, *Galicia Martir,* done by the Spanish artist Alfonso Rodríguez Castelao, which he had with him in Madrid the year before. One of Castelao's sketches is captioned "It is not corpses they bury, but seed." Since Rolfe saw Rafael Alberti regularly in Madrid, and since they exchanged poems with one another, Rolfe would almost certainly have known Alberti's "You Have Not Fallen" ("It is not death, this sowing. There is a birth pang in your anguish"). He may also have read Francisco Giner's "The World Will Be Ours," whose final lines honor "the seeds our fallen brothers have planted." And perhaps Hemingway in turn, whom Rolfe met and became close friends with in Spain, would have had all these texts in mind when he adapted the metaphor for a piece he did for the February 14, 1939, issue of *New Masses*.[10] So may have Langston Hughes, whose poem "Tomorrow's Seed" was later published in the 1952 anthology *The Heart of Spain*. The metaphor has a longer history, of course, but it grows distinctively in Spanish soil. In any case, in a gesture that echoes through the poetry of the war, Rolfe concludes that this is, after all, no grave but a "plot where the self-growing seed" reaches out to turn the soil over, "ceaselessly growing."[11]

In this, as in everything else in the poem, Rolfe writes Reid's epitaph in the light of his representative sacrifice. What testifies to their personal history is not the recitation of intimate detail—for there is none in the poem—but rather the decision to write the poem at the site of Reid's freshly dug grave, the choice of Reid as the embodiment of the commitment to Spain. Late in 1938 Rolfe wrote to Joseph Freeman, who had published a letter about Reid in *New Masses* in September: "Your letter on Arnold was good. I wish I hadn't felt that I had to throttle all personal feeling in my own dispatch."[12] Yet Rolfe's *New Masses* "dispatch" is actually relatively personal, very personal, certainly, in comparison with his poem "Epitaph." No such second thoughts, notably, occur about the poem in any of his diaries or letters; he simply does not think of poetry as an appropriate vehicle for autobiography or unmediated self-expression. It is rather the place where personal experience is to be transmuted into epiphanic historical testimony.

"Political Prisoner 123456789" is from the dark days of the postwar suppression of free speech in America. The title's serial recitation of the first nine numbers signals several things at once: the relentless accumulation of the inquisition's victims, the way that incarceration obliterates their individual differences, and the paradoxical interchangeability of their personal suffering. It is the shared, characteristic, but individually felt and lived reality of their stories that the poem itself then takes up. "I have heard this man called traitor," Rolfe writes, "I saw him shamed / before his friends . . . the walls of his few rooms torn wide for all to see." Although we can read the poem as speaking for all the political prisoners of its time and read it so that it continues to speak for the political prisoners of our time as well, it really addresses those who have been unjustly imprisoned. There is a risk, then, in overly idealizing and universalizing its referent. Hidden beneath the anonymity of the poem's object, moreover, is a different and more specific form of testimony. For one of Rolfe's friends has told us that it was the Hollywood Ten, several of them close friends of Rolfe's—in federal prison for standing up for their constitutional rights—that he had in mind.[13] The title in fact was to be "Political Prisoner 12345678910." But one of the ten, Edward Dmytryk, recanted and cooperated with the House Un-American Activities Committee.[14] He is thus effectively excluded from the poem's title. And the poem testifies—by that silence—to the shock of that betrayal and to the moral standards incumbent upon victims of oppression. As Rolfe makes clear here and in other poems, it is not, finally, his position that there can be no traitors, rather that these nine men were not.

If all these poems are about Rolfe's friends, if they are all written out of personal experience, their testimony on that level is either indirect or elided. For both Rolfe and the people who become subjects of these poems are positioned primarily as subjects of history. Part of what one can regain by recovering some of the biographical background to the poems is a sense of how Rolfe typically deals with material from his life; writing a poem for him is partly a matter of deciding how to handle biographical materials at the politically pertinent distance. The people in Rolfe's poems most often live as agents within history, and when they act—because action *is* possible—they often pay the price the times exact for their agency. The ways contemporary history plays itself out in people's lives and the ways people take up public issues in their beliefs and actions are Rolfe's most pressing subjects. Of course he sometimes writes about himself, but generally he treats himself as a historical subject as well.

Not all his poems include the sort of largely hidden personal references I have noted above, though it is now too late to know for certain how many do. One would not know from his poem on Chaplin, "The Melancholy Comus," that Rolfe and Chaplin were friends. And one would not know that when Rolfe was in the hospital he dreamed once that Chaplin visited him there. The poem takes up the public Chaplin with obvious affection—"Because he is what we would be / we love him"—and it does so in part because Rolfe felt Chaplin's public trial by the media as the harrowing of a friend. But Rolfe aims to draw on those personal feelings to augment and deepen the public Chaplin we all can know:

> The poem finds in the figure of Chaplin an embodiment of physical and emotional contradictions—the tiny hat perched awkwardly on his head, the too-small vest, the overlarge pants, and the enormous shoes are external manifestations of the complexity of the character's psyche. These are the contradictions that define us. When the speaker says "our own feet ache in his comic shoes," he reminds us we are like Chaplin, an "authentic mystery." "Our loneliness from which there is no escape" is in this vision both what makes us individuals and part of what ties us to each other as a society. It is a subtle joke to say that our own feet ache in his comic shoes, since the problem of Chaplin's shoes is that they are too large, not too small. What "pinches" us in our subjectivity is not its narrowness but its wideness; the ache is nothing less than the self's social relations. Chaplin symbolizes a certain reconciliation of all these discontinuities: "In him, blended perfectly, are man, woman, child." Our feet ache in his shoes, ironically, because they are so hard to fill.[15]

In the case of "The Melancholy Comus" Rolfe carefully writes a public poem grounded in unacknowledged personal affection. Yet personal associations are not the only kinds of information virtually erased in Rolfe's work.

One might conclude from the overridingly clear and consistent thematics of his three books that Rolfe's historical references are readily available to the reader. Often they are. Certainly long descriptive or narrative poems like "City of Anguish" give a rather full sense of the historical conditions they seek to evoke. The poems in each of the sections of *Trees Became Torches,* moreover, reinforce one another and fill out each other's historical contexts. But Rolfe's poems also contain a significant number of almost fatalistically abbreviated historical references. How many readers will remember the German anarchist writer Erich Muehsam when they read the phrase "Nazi faces murdering Muehsam" in the poem "May 22nd 1939"? How many will catch the allusion to the Czarist-era Pale of Settlement in the phrase "the colorless Pale" in "Now the Fog"? In a very real sense the poems themselves are written in exile from their proper audience, an audience for whom all these references are resonant.

Rolfe thus knew that many of these allusions would pass unrecognized. Superficially, the tactic of including fragmentary historical references in a modern poem seems Poundian. But with Pound we know that every historical reference has been taken up in the synthesis effected by one idiosyncratic ego; the only real significance of these bits of history lies in what they meant to Pound. Rolfe, however, often testified instead to the pathos of the now culturally decathected material facts themselves. It is almost as if the more fragmentary references can testify only to their absence from common knowledge; by the time we read the poems certain names have been cast already into a void of forgotten time. Rolfe knew he could not keep all these names within a network of shared meanings; all the poem can guarantee is their audibility. They are thus, in effect, vanishing citations, testimony at once to the forgetfulness that dominates historical memory and to a fatalistic recognition that a poem can never contain everything we need to know in order to interpret it.

Not uncommonly, writing such poems for Rolfe is partly a way of coming to terms with difficult historically representative experience and of asking what can be learned of it that might be useful for the rest of us. Thus when Rolfe was unjustly slandered at the *Daily Worker* in 1934 and fired as a result, he turned to poetry to make some sense of the experience.[16] The result is one of his most well-known early poems, "Definition," in which he acknowledges that some who are underhanded and some who are fools will choose to be called comrade, but argues that the ideals underlying the word cannot be compromised that way. Hailed as a comrade by one deficient in these values, he will nevertheless "answer the salutation proudly," thereby honoring the ideal. Nearly twenty years later, in May 1952, he turned on the radio and learned that his friend

Clifford Odets has just betrayed himself and his friends by testifying before the House Un-American Activities Committee. Rolfe turned from the radio and in a few hours drafted a new poem, first calling it "Ballad of the Lost Friend" and later retitling it "Ballad of the Noble Intentions," thereby again making the poem more representative than personal.[17] It is a ballad structured as a dialogue, a kind of witty and anguished mock interrogation, as Rolfe adopts the committee's question-and-answer method with different aims—to search for the truth rather than for lies. "What will you do, my brother, my friend, / when they summon you to their inquisition," he asks, "And what will you say, my brother, my friend, / when they threaten your family's food instead?" The form, of course, has obvious risks, since the speaker is effectively conducting his own interrogation. It works only because Rolfe also enters into the inner world of painful self-justification that unwilling witnesses had to create for themselves. The answers are not sufficient to save this speaker's honor—indeed, Odets, as it happened, unlike some other witnesses, tortured himself about his testimony—but it is only in the last four (out of nineteen) stanzas that Rolfe's judgment is set: "Your act of survival betrayed *not* your friends, / but yourself. . . . And *that* was your crime; in the noon of your life / you resigned from the living."

At every point Rolfe imagined such poems not simply as detached comments about events but as events themselves, as interventions in social and political life. He wanted poems to empower readers who shared his beliefs—giving them language and speaking positions they might need but be unable to articulate on their own—and to challenge and persuade those who disagreed with him. Both groups, moreover, were asked to take on complications not always typical of political dialogue. Rolfe also clearly believed that poetry has distinctive cultural work to do. For him, poetry was not interchangeable with other forms of persuasion. More than any other kind of writing, it could succinctly capture what was most critical in the dynamics of lived history. If poetry for Rolfe was effectively the soul of an age, that means it could record the essential character of history, not that it could exit history and transcend it.

Accomplishing this sort of work meant taking on poetry as a deliberate craft. These poems are not for the most part composed of the sort of political rhetoric that can come easily in daily speech. Although Rolfe sometimes wrote and published poems immediately after the events they describe, he also revised poems extensively, occasionally working on them for years, and his revisions consistently sharpen his language and make his metaphors more distinctive. In some ways, indeed, his methods are quite traditional; a number of his drafts, for example, have been carefully scanned, the stresses noted and counted. If the image of a revolutionary poet studiously monitoring rhyme and meter is surprising, so be it. If it seems improbable or contradictory, perhaps that is because we have forgotten what social and political functions poetry has served in the past and may yet serve again in the future. For the last five decades in America many of us have held an image of political poetry as automatic and unreflective. Yet the historical record is actually quite different from that.

For a time, Rolfe had some real cultural support in the role of revolutionary poet. He rarely had much time to write poetry, to be sure, since he generally earned his living as a journalist, but at least he was recognized as a notable young poet. When *To My Contemporaries* was published, it received some of the attention it merited as a distinctive contribution to a major cultural movement. Horace Gregory provided the book's jacket comment and selected Rolfe as the lead poet of the social poets issue he guest edited for *Poetry* in May 1936. A few months later, in the July issue of *Poetry*, Harriet Monroe described him as "the best among these inflammatory young men and women." That year the *New York Times Book Review* reviewed Rolfe along with Kenneth Patchen and Stanley Burnshaw under the heading "Three Young Marxist Poets" and declared him "one of the best of these younger poets." Rolfe's photograph was published on the first page of the review. The *New Yorker* declared him "If not the most flowery, perhaps the most readable and sincere of the poets of the Left." Morton Dauwen Zabel, in an omnibus review in the *Southern Review*, ranked him the best among five radical American poets. More detailed commentaries appeared by Joseph Freeman in *New Masses* and by Kenneth Fearing in the *Daily Worker*. It was partly that reputation—as well as his credentials as a Left journalist—that led Bennett Cerf to sign him on two years later to do the first history of the Lincoln Battalion. Yet *To My Contemporaries* would be the only time Rolfe received widespread attention for one of his books of poetry. Ironically, his later work was more rhetorically accomplished, but by then the dominant culture had scandalized and excommunicated everything that mattered to him, and Rolfe's subsequent books of poetry went mostly unnoticed in the major reviewing media.

When *To My Contemporaries* was published in 1936, Rolfe had been living with Mary Wolfe for nearly two years, and they were married that fall. Mary had also grown up in New York on the Left and was also a Party member, so they shared not only their personal lives but also the social and political life of the next two decades. Their life together, however, was soon to be transformed by events in Europe, for in the summer of 1936 the Spanish Civil War began, and Rolfe's thoughts soon turned to Spain.

No cause in the 1930s had quite the power of the international effort to come to the defense of the Spanish republic. From the outset, when a group of right-wing army officers revolted against the elected Popular Front Coalition government in July 1936, it was clear that Spain was to be at once the real and symbolic site of the growing struggle between democracy and fascism. Mussolini's Italy may have begun to work on behalf of the army officers even before the revolt began, and Franco secured the cooperation of Hitler's Germany within a week. The Western democracies, unfortunately, assumed a noninterventionist policy, partly on the deluded hope that such a stance would discourage German and Italian 'participation and partly because some in the West were more comfortable with a fascist government in Spain than with an elected government whose policies were disturbingly progressive. Only the Soviet Union regularly made limited arms available for sale to the Spanish government. As a result the Loyalist troops were often undersupplied and poorly armed. But their cause drew support from the broadest possible international coalition. "Spain," Rolfe proclaimed in a poem written during the war, "is yesterday's Russia, tomorrow's China, / yes and the thirteen seaboard states."

At first there was no organized effort to solicit foreign volunteers. But people recognizing the great danger of fascism and people sympathetic with the Left soon began crossing the border into Spain to offer what help they could; most entered Spain through France, but they came from Britain and from all across Europe. This remarkable phenomenon—a mixture of selfless idealism and historical insight—helped galvanize the international Left. Soon the Comintern (Communist International) decided to organize groups of international volunteers and to make travel arrangements for them; Spain in turn set up formal training bases in small towns near Albacete, which was the administrative center for the brigades. By that time some volunteers had already seen action, but the first battle in which the International Brigades themselves made a major contribution was the historic struggle for Madrid that November. Franco attacked the city in force, hoping to take the capital and end the war swiftly. But the people of Madrid built barricades, organized to fight, and the city held. The fascist offensive was broken in dramatic battles that included hand-to-hand combat in the city's suburbs. For five months Madrid and the surrounding towns would be the main strategic goal of the rebel troops.

It took Rolfe some time to get permission to join the volunteers, but in

June 1937 he hiked across the Pyrenees Mountains and was shortly in train-
ing at Tarazona. By that time the International Brigades were issuing a regular
newspaper in several languages out of their Madrid offices. The novelist Ralph
Bates, who was editing the English-language version of *Volunteer for Liberty,*
was scheduled to leave Spain. After training for a month to join a fighting
unit, Rolfe was offered Bates's job. Rolfe refused, but his extensive experience
as a journalist made him an obvious choice, so the offer was soon changed
to an order. The job of editing the newspaper brought him back to the front
regularly, and he assumed other responsibilities as well: serving as political
commissar in Madrid and organizing shortwave radio broadcasts.

   With the front only two kilometers away, Madrid was very much a city
under siege. Food was limited and several times a week the rebel guns on
Mount Garabitas shelled the city. In the downtown section hundreds of civil-
ians were regularly killed or wounded. Consistent with the paradoxical inten-
sity of a city at war, the experience felt alternately theatrical and terrifying.
At night, Rolfe and other Madrileños sometimes watched the bombardments
from rooftops. But there was also continual surreal violence and appalling
human tragedy. The bombings took their place in the poems he began to write.
It took some time to complete his long poem "City of Anguish," first simply
called "Madrid," but on August 3 he began working on it, writing four pages
about the previous night's bombardment:

> The headless body
> stands strangely, totters for a second, falls.
> The girl speeds screaming through wreckage; her hair is
> wilder than torture.
> The solitary foot,
> deep-arched, is perfect on the cobbles, naked,
> strong, ridged with strong veins, upright, complete . . .
> The city weeps. The city shudders, weeping.

   Exploiting the literariness of poetic language, as Rolfe does here, has obvi-
ous risks when the subject is violence. If the ironies of a violence transfigured,
beatified by literariness, cannot be entirely controlled, however, they can at
least be clearly bound to their context. "City of Anguish" is one of Rolfe's most
elaborate efforts in that direction. Here he makes it clear that part of the city's
anguish is the transfiguration of its mental life. He specifies not only the vio-
lence that he sees but also the violence he imagines. Madrid is a city where "soil

and stone / spilled like brains from the sandbag's head." "The mind," he writes, "calculates destruction" whether we will it to or not. Part of what he commemorates here, just as he commemorates heroism in battle in other poems, is the special beauty of Madrid under siege. Yet in Rolfe's poetry it is possible to be drawn to the surreal beauty of these images without feeling that their horror is undercut.

At other times, like some of the other poets who wrote about Spain, Rolfe preferred a more straightforward polemicism. At such points he did not want his moral aims subverted by the duplicities of explicit metaphorization. He is also, however, capable of taking on the ambiguities of metaphoric language while retaining clear moral and political perspectives. "Come for a joyride in Madrid," he urges us, but don't count yourself as having had the full experience until you've heard "the zoom of / planes like a ferris wheel strafing the trenches": "War is your comrade struck dead beside you, / his shared cigarette still alive in your lips."

As these lines suggest, while Madrid suffered Rolfe also had to deal with another kind of death, not so visible as the bodies he saw in the streets, but because of that distance perhaps still more painful—the deaths of his comrades in the battalion. Sometimes he simply sat down to record the names of the dead and wounded in his diary. A September 13 entry includes the lines "Sidney Shosteck dead—shot between eyes by a sniper's bullet while bringing a tank in. Danny Hutner also dead." The same day he wrote home about Shosteck's death, reporting that they had met during training and that Shosteck visited him in Madrid. A week later, on September 20, he wrote "Elegy for Our Dead," which he dedicated to Shosteck and Hutner and eventually published in the *Volunteer*. A number of the poems of the last month remained as yet in unfinished drafts; this is the first finished poem about Spain that fully satisfied him. And it is his effort to make an enduring historical statement about what is distinctive about these comrades he had lost there. As he noted in his diary, the "poem was not meant to be, but turned out to be," at least in part, "an answer to Rupert Brooke's 'corner that is forever England'"; this time the dead honor something larger than nationalism.

That August and September of 1937 in Madrid he also drafted several of the other poems about Spain, including "Eyes of a Boy" and "Eyes of a Blind Man," which he wrote on September 6, after meeting Commandante Fort of the Franco-Belge Battalion; Fort was blinded at Brunete in July. "Death by Water," a poem about a steamship carrying volunteers that is torpedoed off the coast of Malgrat, is of special note because of its explicit reference to

Eliot. Although Rolfe's first title was "City of Barcelona," his direct quotation of Eliot's phrase "the cry of gulls" in his first line makes it clear that he had the fourth section of *The Waste Land* in mind from the outset. "Death by Water," is, of course, the shortest and most unqualifiedly mythic section of Eliot's poem. So Rolfe's poem—which is about real people who die within history because of their political commitments—directly confronts the mythic tendency within high modernism with his own convictions about historical specificity. The second stanza invokes Coleridge's "The Rime of the Ancient Mariner" to reject another kind of allusive mythologizing as well: the albatross is superseded by "the vultures descending on an Ethiopian plain," recalling Mussolini's invasion of North Africa. All this sets us up for the sudden shock of the torpedo exploding against the steamship in the next stanza.

Throughout this time Rolfe felt deeply troubled at being relatively safe in Madrid. In January 1938, the International Brigades offices were moved to Barcelona. That spring the order came through for all able-bodied men to leave for the front. It was not supposed to apply to Rolfe, but he decided to act on it anyway and joined the battalion in the field in April. He participated in the Ebro campaign, which included the largest battles of the war, and soon after that was asked to take over for Joe North as Spanish correspondent for the *Daily Worker* and *New Masses*.

When Rolfe returned from Spain in January 1939 the Loyalist cause was already under attack. Martin Dies had begun congressional hearings on Communist activity, and people who had worked on Spain's behalf were under suspicion. Rolfe's brother Bern, a federal employee who had raised funds for Loyalist Spain, was among those who came under scrutiny, though he would keep his government job for a time. In any case, it was clear that the Left was in for some difficulty, though it seemed then that the Left would be strong enough to defend itself successfully. Still, it was deeply disturbing to watch heroes of the war like Milt Wolff harassed in front of the House Un-American Activities Committee. For much of the next two years, then, Spain remained at the center of Rolfe's life. He signed a contract to write a history of the Lincolns, and late in 1939 Random House brought it out under the title *The Lincoln Battalion*. That July he also finished the striking but uncollected poem "Paris—Christmas 1938," first calling it "Lullaby," and later that year drafted a version of "Brigadas Internacionales," his brief, ringing proclamation of the justice of the Spanish cause, a poem that should be read in its context, as a principled defense of a cause under assault.

Rolfe's life in the meantime took unexpected directions. Once *The Lincoln*

Battalion was done, he had to face the difficulty of finding work again. In March 1940 he took a job as an editor at the New York office of Tass, the Soviet News Agency, which employed several Spanish Civil War vets at the time. Although he managed to attend meetings of the Veterans of the Abraham Lincoln Brigade, Tass otherwise required him to avoid political activities. Unfortunately, they also prohibited employees from publishing independently. Rolfe thus could not publish his poetry for several years, not until he was drafted into the U.S. Army and resigned from Tass in 1943.

Rolfe became ill while in training at Camp Wolters in Texas and was discharged, but not before he had a chance to see the difference between the deeply committed volunteers in Spain and the young recruits in Texas. Two poems from that spring and summer in Texas are of special importance. In May, borrowing his title from William Vaughan Moody's turn-of-the-century anti-imperialist poem against our war in the Philippines, Rolfe wrote "In the Time of Hesitation," in which he describes the historical forces requiring that these boys be turned into soldiers while realizing that they have little awareness of recent history. Spain is already disappearing from the popular memory.

Thus Rolfe did not leave the army before historicizing his situation in a more profound and problematic way. For a series of recognitions converged on him in Texas. It was partly the sharp realization of his generational difference and partly as well the specific social and political commitments, the very distinctive camaraderie, he witnessed in Spain but missed among the young men and officers around him in Texas. Training to fight in Texas, he could not help recalling that he had fought five years earlier with very different passions and out of an articulate sense of history and history's entanglements that had little equivalent among the draftees he met here. If the cultural environment he was part of was improbable and the immediate audience for his writing at best surreal, he nonetheless did begin to write again. It may be that the alternating heat and rain in Texas were not altogether unlike the seasonal extremes on the plains at Tarazona. When he left the army, he would begin theorizing the differences between these two wars in prose. But for now these issues coalesced and found expression in poetry.

"In the Time of Hesitation" was the first realization of his double consciousness. There is the dust of these plains, he observes, the dust in the ruins of Spain, and the dust that individual memory faces if it is not recorded. And of course, always in the background is the famous passage from the service for the burial of the dead in *The Book of Common Prayer:* "ashes to ashes, dust to dust." Rolfe concludes with a reflection on the necessity of turning these children rapidly into "men or corpses." For "the world cannot wait." Some, to be sure, await the invasion of Europe; others await the opening of that second front that will deflect some of the pressure of the German attack on the Soviet Union; it is a difference temporarily to be set aside. But Rolfe is not yet satisfied with his rendering of the meaning of Spain remembered on the possible eve of a return to arms in Europe.

Under the pressure to give witness to that renewed memory, something changes in the rhetoric available to him. His poetry undergoes a shift in compression and metaphoric complexity. And in the heat of Texas he writes what will be his signature poem, "First Love," a haunting and lyrical tribute to Spain's hold on him and a poem that, while politicizing a romantic trope, also insists that the passionate core of his politics remains a permanent resource:

> Again I am summoned to the eternal field
> green with the blood still fresh at the roots of flowers,
> green through the dust-rimmed memory of faces
> that moved among the trees there for the last time
> before the final shock, the glazed eye, the hasty mound.
>
> But why are my thoughts in another country?
> Why do I always return to the sunken road through corroded
>   hills,
> with the Moorish castle's shadow casting ruins over my
>   shoulder
> and the black-smocked girl approaching, her hands laden
>   with grapes?
>
> I am eager to enter it, eager to end it.
> Perhaps this will be the last one.
> And men afterward will study our arms in museums
> and nod their heads, and frown, and name the inadequate dates
> and stumble with infant tongues over the strange place-names.
>
> But my heart is forever captive of that other war
> that taught me first the meaning of peace and of
>   comradeship
> and always I think of my friend who amid the apparition of
>   bombs
> saw on the lyric lake the single perfect swan.

As Karen Ford has written persuasively about this love poem to Spain, "contrary to what we might expect, the romantic suggestiveness of the title 'First Love' is not exposed in the poem as a subjective, idealized illusion that the grim brutality and grave morality of war must embarrass. Instead, the poem insists that the intense subjectivity of romantic love and the daunting generality of social struggle are connected, though their connection must constantly be scrutinized to assure that each term is held up for measure by the other."[18] As she adds about one of the poem's more haunting images,

> that war makes love central to Rolfe's ideals is expressed in the image of the Spanish girl, who embodies both love and death: "the black-smocked girl approaching, her hands laden with grapes." The girl is clearly a reaper (she carries the grapes she has picked) and probably a grim reaper (the black smock, however traditional, nonetheless suggests this), but she is also a figure of innocence (she is just a girl) and vitality (she is young and holds the bacchanalian grapes). The approach of death makes love urgent because it forces us to decide what in our lives is most important. She is Spain personified as an exotic yet innocent woman; as such, she is an instance of the poem's irreducibly inaugural and retrospective title. What Rolfe wants from this and many other invocations of romantic love is both a paradigm of human relations and a source of energy—emotional and erotic—that can be tapped for revolutionary purposes.

Here in America, then, in the heat of our southern plains, still he finds Spain present to his mind and central to his life. And there is a reason why this is true, beyond the accidents of circumstance and the politics of commitment that brought him to Madrid and to the hills above the Ebro River. For at the core of the Spanish experience were a set of values and a vision of human perfectibility within history that are quite different from the need, however real, to put an end to Hitler and Mussolini.

That is not to say that "First Love" has no relevance to other historical moments and to other people's lives. The poem would have resonance for anyone training to fight in a second war amongst younger recruits with no comparable experience. Certainly the pathos of the "strange place-names" that enter public discourse during a foreign war only to be widely forgotten shortly thereafter, meanwhile remaining resonant or even pivotal for those who fought there, is a pathos any veteran will understand—as indeed will anyone who has lived long enough to see crucial historical events become irrelevant to younger generations. Rolfe himself calls the field of battle "green with the blood still fresh at the roots of flowers" an "eternal" one. But in fact he means that field to have other connotations as well: it is the field of specific memories that hold fresh for him, and those memories are eternal not so much in their applicability to other struggles as in their singularity. The selfless gift of those international volunteers who went to the aid of the Spanish republic—a gift whose purity remains a resource to succeeding generations—is part of what justifies the assertion that there were flowers on those battlefields, flowers that thus signify more than the ordinary disruption of a pastoral setting by war or the flowers at a soldier's grave.

Despite Franco's victory, despite the subsequent red-baiting of those who went to Spain, the dream and the trauma of Spain remain unsullied. The last stanza, with its self-declared lyricism, makes that claim explicit. A biographical incident lies behind these lines, but it emerges in the poem not as autobiography but as a lyrical emblem. When a train full of American volunteers was scheduled to leave Spain, Rolfe and the correspondent Vincent Sheean were among others there at Puigcerdá to see them off. As it happened, the train arrived and left early, and it was well it did, for at the scheduled arrival two squadrons of Franco's planes flew over and bombed the station heavily. They thus missed their intended target, and that group of internationals left safely. Shortly thereafter, Sheean saw one swan on a nearby lake and remarked the contrast to Rolfe.[19] Here, however, Rolfe raises the image to a more general meaning. For it is the special justice of the Spanish cause—its moral specificity as a historical event—that justifies the lyrical vision at the poem's end. If it is thus an explicit triumph of literariness, it is not an exclusively textual one. Rolfe's point is that the poetic lyricism is historically warranted.

By the time Rolfe left the army that summer, his wife, Mary, had accepted a job administering the Left-oriented writer's school established in Los Angeles by the League of American Writers. Rolfe left New York to join her after a few days and remained in California for the rest of his life. He began to work on the manuscript that would become *First Love,* meanwhile writing a number of short stories and finding a little work on the fringes of the motion picture industry. Late in 1945 he finished a coauthored mystery novel, *The Glass Room,* the film rights for which were purchased by Warner Brothers. Industry newspapers announced that Bogart and Bacall had been signed to play the leads, and it looked like Rolfe might finally have some financial security. History intervened, however, in the form of the blacklist, and plans for the film were dropped.

In 1947 anticommunism, in remission during the war when we were allies with the Soviet Union, returned to function much more effectively and per-vasively than it had before. A vast confederation of repressive forces—from national, state, and local government to the media, business leaders, and politi-cal organizations—collected around economic and political interests that had much to gain from instituting and maintaining the cold war. Business interests found Communist conspiracy theories the best way to win consent to continue the profitable war economy and the best way as well to break those unions that remained strong and uncooperative during and after the war. Opportunist politicians with little national following found theatrically staged anticommu-nist hearings an easy way to build reputations. A group of reactionary political organizations whose members actually believed the well-publicized stories of Communist subversion—from the American Legion to the Daughters of the American Revolution—offered enthusiastic support. In the end, some people on the Left went to jail and many thousands lost their jobs. There was a nationwide purge from all public and much private employment not only of Communist party members but also of anyone with any history of support for the Left.

Rolfe saw his friends amongst the Hollywood Ten go to prison, including Alvah Bessie, a fellow Lincoln Battalion veteran. A number of party officials also fought losing battles through the courts. Efforts were under way to de-port some of his exiled comrades and force them to return to Spain and certain death, and the blacklist destroyed the careers of most of his Hollywood friends.

In this gathering atmosphere of repression, Rolfe turned one last time to write of Spain. As early as 1939 he had planned a long narrative poem about Spain focused on the international volunteers. It would include a history of the major military actions—from Jarama through Brunete and Teruel to the Ebro—and first-person narratives of some of those who died. His typed out-line begins with a definition of "the *spine* of the poem: that hope for men exists in the survival of such qualities which (whether the Spanish government is finally defeated or not) has been proved by her defenders. In this poem the stress will be on the International Brigades, and specifically the Americans in the Brigades. The qualities: courage, conviction deep enough to move men, voluntarily, from safety and comparative security to field of battle; clarity, hope, deepest kind of human dignity." He also planned a long poem from the per-spective of a Spanish peasant on the Loyalist side. It was to be the young man's story of the struggle over his village, Segura de los Baños, as it was captured by the enemy, freed by his people, and finally taken again by the National-ist troops.[20] Rolfe drew a picture of the town, modeled partly on Tarazona de la Mancha and Federally, and wrote a prologue to the poem: "My village rose along the side of a hill, terrace above terrace, to a point midway between the miniature valley and the pine-scrub dotted peak of Sierra Pedigrossa. You would not find it on any map; it is too small—perhaps 100 clay and stone cottages for men and women and children, and another fifty stone and adobe huts for the animals. Yet my village is important—it is the exact center of all space and all time." Neither of these poems would end up being written.

In 1948, when he turned to Spain for the last time, it was the status of the memory within the battalion and amongst Spanish exiles that most needed retelling. As he had with "City of Anguish," Rolfe chose again to focus on Madrid. As Aaron Kramer would write in a review in the January 16, 1952, issue of *National Guardian,* "into this love-song to Madrid, written ten years after his return, Rolfe pours all the emotion he'd been holding back for so long. . . . Paraphrasing the 137th Psalm, that unforgettable love-song to Jerusalem chanted once by the rivers of Babylon, Rolfe sings 'If I die before I can return to you . . . my sons will love you as their father did.'" Now, by the waters of an American Babylon, marginalized on a Left under increasing assault, Rolfe calls on the memory of the great city under siege that had been the heart of the world. Madrid would be a figure not only for what might have been but also for a common cause, a successful alliance politics, that only weeks before had come unraveled in America precisely when it was most needed. Thus Madrid in 1948 would be a figure for an idealism and solidarity not so much imperiled as near extinction:

> Madrid   Madrid   Madrid   Madrid
> I call your name endlessly, savor it like a lover.
> Ten irretrievable years have exploded like bombs
> Since last I saw you, since last I slept
> in your arms of tenderness and wounded granite.
> Ten years since I touched your face in the sun,
> ten years since the homeless Guadarrama winds
> moaned like shivering orphans through your veins
> and I moaned with them.
> When I think of you, Madrid,
> locked in the bordello of the Universal Pimp,
> the blood that rushes to my heart and head
> blinds me, and I could strangle your blood-bespattered
>   jailors,

choke them with these two hands which once embraced you.
When I think of your breathing body of vibrancy and sun,
silently I weep, in my own native land
which I love no less because I love you more.
Yet I know, in the heart of my heart, that until your
    liberation
rings through the world of free men near and far
I must wander like an alien everywhere.

Just over 110 lines, "Elegia" was Rolfe's last great poem about Spain. It was written the year after Alvah Bessie and others were called before HUAC to testify as punishment for their long commitment to the Left. From 1936 to 1939 something like a chorus of voices called back and forth to each other about the besieged city of Madrid. In poem after poem in country after country the name *Madrid* is used as a rallying cry and an incantation, sometimes with and sometimes without an exclamation mark. The poems echo one another across time and space and national or political difference, ring changes on the suffering and courage of the Madrileños, and establish in print, in voice, and in dream and nightmare the point of articulation of an antifascist politics for its time. Now in 1948 Rolfe prints the name repeatedly to form his opening line. There is no punctuation in the opening line, and an extra space falls between each recitation of the city's name. Into each of those spaces ten years fall. Across each of those spaces reaches an unanswered yearning for the lost community of the Left.

The lyricism of the opening lines has won readers to the poem ever since it was published. And it would be easy for those of us steeped in the New Critical taste of the last five decades to conclude that Rolfe succeeds in such lyrical moments and fails when his language is more worldly, brutal, or hortatory. Thus among Rolfe's Spain poems the lyrical "First Love" would meet with our approval and the declamatory "Brigadas Internacionales" would not. These two stanzas from "Elegia" provide a good place to test that sort of perspective because the first stanza is more explicitly lyrical and the second more angry and rhetorical. But the two stanzas are not mutually exclusive stylistically. The two tendencies invade one another, suggesting that that these two discursive registers—lyricism and polemicism—are actually interdependent. Thus the ten years that have "exploded like bombs" cannot be purely metaphoric in the context of a city that was the scene of massive bombardment; the metaphor slips over into real violence. Similarly, the more lyrical notes in the second stanza—

the reference to Madrid's "breathing body of vibrancy and sun" and the concluding reference to the enforced diaspora of the Loyalist alliance—are colored by anger at the fascist victory that keeps the speaker distant. Rolfe, we realize, is not interested in indulging himself in a transcendentalizing lyricism but rather in displaying a lyrical impulse that is itself historically occasioned and necessarily in dialogue with other kinds of language. We have become accustomed to thinking of poetry as a space where lyricism can be entertained for its own sake, but Rolfe is not willing to pursue lyricism as an independent cultural value. Even in shorter poems he is unwilling to give himself or his readers over to an unselfconscious lyricism. Indeed, whether Rolfe's different styles compete within individual poems or coalesce in poems dominated by one style or another, their effects remain relational. These styles, moreover, enable poetry to do different kinds of cultural work. Recognizing that makes it possible to value both "First Love" and "Brigadas Internacionales." Failing to recognize that, moreover, means maintaining an impoverished view of a poem like "Elegia."

Indeed, it may be that Rolfe never wrote a poem that does not in some way problematize its lyrical language. Even in "First Love" he carefully disturbs and compromises the more overtly poetic diction and rhythms. Thus the lyrical first stanza—troubled early on by the surreal assertion that the field is *green* with fresh blood, diction that may recall García Lorca—is then three times abruptly terminated in its final line: "the final shock, the glazed eye, the hasty mound." These three phrases also compress a narrative sequence into three brutal photographs—a soldier is hit and killed; the glazed eyes of his corpse stare emptily at the sky; the hasty mound is a burial site in the field. He returns in the second stanza to lines more reassuring lyrical, but even there inserts the beautiful but aurally difficult image of "the Moorish castle's shadow." Throughout, as in so much of Rolfe's poetry, evocative specific description ("the sunken road through corroded hills") sits near relatively flat abstraction ("the meaning of peace and of comradeship"). And even the most memorable lyrical effects are realized with relatively unadorned diction. In "First Love," the epiphanic final image is inseparable from a number of willfully self-conscious effects, including the insistent alliteration of "lyric lake" and the off-rhyme of "bombs" and "swan." Similar complications run through the entirety of a long poem like "Elegia."

When Rolfe wrote "Elegia" there was literally no place to publish it. Even the Commmunist party–supported *Masses and Mainstream* refused it, in part because the biblical allusions offended the editors; religion, after all, could only be the opiate of the people. It was one more piece of foolishness from the Party, but Rolfe would not break the commitment to communism he had first made in 1925. Still, it was singularly painful to have his lamentation and love song for Madrid silenced. But his friend the Spanish exile José Rubia Barcia, under attack from the U.S. immigration service, translated the poem into Spanish and sent it to the filmmaker Luis Buñuel, who gave it to a mutual friend, the well-known Spanish poet and printer Manuel Altolaguirre, living in exile in Mexico City. Altolaguirre, one of the key Republican poets during the war, was so moved that he set the poem in type and printed it as a pamphlet without charge.[21] Circulated throughout Latin America, it was read out loud in meetings of Spanish exiles in Argentina, Chile, and Mexico, one last gift from a member of the International Brigades to his Spanish comrades. In 1950 Rolfe sent the poem to Hemingway, who replied in April: "Got back four days ago and just found your letter and fine ELEGIA. . . . Your fucking poem made me cry and I have only cried maybe four times in my life which is now gone on for half a hundred years and 8 months. If this is any value as literary criticism there she is and how do you like it now, Gentlemen? Anyway the times (five now) I always cried for other people and now for a fucking town."[22]

"Elegia" was not to appear in English until 1951, when Rolfe finally published *First Love and Other Poems* himself; it had become clear that no commercial publisher would touch a book whose commitments were considered heretical. The book opens with some of the poems Rolfe wrote in Spain during the war, including "Casualty," which he wrote in Barcelona on March 17, 1938. It closes with his most lyrical postwar tributes to the memory of Spain. *First Love* is also effectively framed with two long poems—one placed second in the book and one in the penultimate position—"City of Anguish" and "Elegia"— and thus by the name of one city: Madrid.

From this point on, for the last six years of his life, Rolfe wrote largely of repression at home. It is those poems that make up the final section of Rolfe's *Selected Poems*. As he makes clear in a fragment, the poems of these years serve first as a call to his country to look into its own heart:

> Yes, you, my dear friends, fellow-dwellers in my town,
> inventors of hearsay, slanderous tellers of tales,
> assassins whose weapon is nuance, betrayers of friends,
> look into the face of this poem: its features are your own.

Despite the damage done to people's lives, cooperation with HUAC became somewhat ritualized: apologies for earlier radical activities, disavowal of all

Left positions, compliments to the committee on the importance of its work, and, finally, and most importantly, the naming of names. People who were either in the party or fellow travelers were expected to name people they believed to be Communists or sympathetic to Communist causes. Meanwhile, paid informers invented stories to sustain the fictional melodrama of a Communist conspiracy to take over the country by force. In Hollywood, watching the newspapers to see if you were named in testimony was like waiting to see if your name appeared in the obituaries. Once your name was published, you had but a few weeks to decide: hold firm to your principles or testify and name names yourself. As he explains in another unpublished passage, it was those who sacrificed others to save themselves whom Rolfe could not forgive:

> Those I could not forgive
> were not the ones who, tiring in midstream,
> turned frantic back to reach their starting point,
> although the desired and shining shore
> was closer than the one they chose to scramble back to;
> not those who, in the middle of their journey,
> turned sadly back; not those who, weakening,
> equated private guilt with large injustice. . . .
> But those who, turning back, sucked others with them,
> them I could not forgive; nor those who,
> secretly accepting the bribe of coin or conscience,
> sought weakly to lend their treason dignity
> with soothing words, with frightened reasoning—
> whose motives, too transparent, were to please
> their own tormentors—
> these alone
> remain my own
> and all men's enemies.

Several of Rolfe's poems take up the materiality of testimony from different perspectives, most notably "Ballad of the Noble Intentions," "Are You Now or Have You Ever Been," and "Letter to the Denouncers." Material like this, which attacked the committee directly, was almost impossible to publish. *The Nation*, for example, accepted Rolfe's "Ballad of the Noble Intentions" for its December 12, 1953, issue and then backed out, claiming the space had been taken by advertising. They promised its publication in a forthcoming issue, but the poem never appeared. Even the *California Quarterly*, one of the few magazines of the Left, decided not to publish "Little Ballad for Americans—1954," one of Rolfe's poems that takes up the general atmosphere of surveillance and betrayal. Not all the poems of this period, however, address the specific practices of the inquisition. "Words Found on a Cave's Wall" works to name the resources left to the victims of the terror: "we endured in the long darkness, sharing our warmth and our desperate hopes." Some, like "On Rico LeBrun's *Crucifixion*," "The poisoned air befouled the whole decade," and "Now the fog," interrogate the culture as a whole:

> Now the fog falls on the land.
> Imagination's eyes go blind. . . .
> Knaves masqued like sovereigns decree
> what we shall say, listen to, see.
> The habit of slavery, long discarded,
> becomes our normal comfortable suit.

Except for a few magazines on the Left, there were no outlets available for such poems. Even then, the harsher, more sardonic, and unforgiving poems could not be placed. He had a few mainstream successes, but only when the analogies with McCarthyism were oblique enough to be missed by many readers. "A Poem to Delight My Friends Who Laugh at Science-Fiction," published in *Poetry* in 1953, is at the outer edges of that sort of indirect critique, for some readers at the time would have easily recognized the poem's political thrust, though its appearance in numerous anthologies since suggest it is easily decontextualized. The initial inspiration for the poem came from a story on the front page of the *New York Times* on Sunday, September 12, 1948.[23] The opening paragraph read "Fog up the Hudson was held responsible for the death of hundreds of migrating birds that crashed into the Empire State Building early yesterday morning and plummeted to the street or setbacks of the skyscraper." Rolfe took the event as a figure for the times, writing to his brother Bern to say that the poem urges us to "wake up and see how closely life in our neck of the world approximates the so-called fantasies of science fiction; how we head ever-closer to a world in which the only ones left alive will be the 'sullen' soldiers, 'unwilling, puppetlike, directionless.'" In any event it is now not the building but the Empire State itself against which we sacrifice ourselves; "the small birds in their frail and delicate battalions / committed suicide against the Empire State":

> That was the year
> men and women everywhere stopped dying natural deaths.
> The agèd, facing sleep, took poison;

the infant, facing life, died with the mother in
   childbirth;
and the whole wild remainder of the population,
despairing but deliberate, crashed in auto accidents
on roads as clear and uncluttered as ponds.

This is the poem's second stanza, and its last line—with its striking image of mortal roadways as "uncluttered as ponds"—wittily combines malice with pastoralism and reinforces the poem's recurring motifs of nature and culture gone wrong. With their "aerial radar" defective, the eerily technological birds crash like lost bomber battalions. Docked ships are discovered "turned over like harpooned whales." Nature and technology interpenetrate to corrupt one another. The culture of the inquisition is everywhere obscene. "Shrieking *I am the state*," the speaker exclaims in "All Ghouls' Night," another poem written in the midst of America's Walpurgisnacht, "Ghoul unleashed his terror."

As we read through Rolfe's McCarthy era poems we begin to see what a range of voices and styles is necessary to negotiate these oppressive years. Characterizing this period of American history is a nearly impossible task, or at least a task that cannot be done on one occasion but rather must be assayed in multiple ways, by direct assault as well as indirection. Indeed, as the first stanza of "In Praise Of" suggests, the intensified knowledge such a task requires is itself nearly disabling. In the end Rolfe wrote both poems indicting the inquisition and poems honoring those ruined by it. There are also poems describing the culture of suspicion—"lighted continents / where privacy is publicly outlawed," a country ruled by those with "the strength / to kill all thought," where "all the bright awards" are "bestowed by coward on his fellow coward" and "where even an innocent unguarded eye / means sudden expulsion." In many of these poems the most difficult effort is to find a rhetoric and a voice that can sustain itself in the presence of impossibly contested emotions. In "Little Ballad for Americans—1954" the wit is inseparable from rage and anguish. "Are You Now or Have You Ever Been" intervenes in the persona of a man testifying before HUAC with a relentlessly unstable mix of irony and self-abasement.

More than once in these years he thinks back to the deaths of Sacco and Vanzetti to make sense of the continuities in his own history and the history he has witnessed:

I think of two men who were murdered
Twenty-three years ago, this very day—
Whose death was my first real introduction to life—

life as my land and my century know it—
Sacco the shoemaker, Vanzetti the seller of fish,
the vendor of human ideas in the market place.

He pairs the deaths of Sacco and Vanzetti with the death of Federico García
Lorca, "the murdered soul of Spain." With these victims linking Spain and
America, linking the martyred poet García Lorca—very much a people's poet
but not a political figure until his death made him one—with two articulate and
politically committed working-class heroes, he draws a circle that is sufficient
to define the historical ground of his work.

This unfinished poem about Sacco and Vanzetti and García Lorca was writ-
ten in 1950 while Rolfe was in a veterans' hospital in Los Angeles recovering
from his third heart attack, his first two having occurred in 1944. He was thus
very much aware that he could not count on living a great deal longer and
inclined to think of beginnings and endings. Looking back on several decades
of writing revolutionary poetry and of the lived history that occasioned it, he
reflected both in prose and in numerous unfinished poems on the continuities
and limits of his craft and on his own mortality. He realized that he had seen
people's scattered discontent and their sense of hopeless disenfranchisement
turned by poetry into an articulate anger. He had seen poetry's startling singu-
larity—paradoxically—empower people to become part of a community. He
had heard poetry focus the will to change and give lyrical voice to irremediable
loss. He had known people to take up a poem's voice as their own and—at
least for a moment—live as though its form were their own body. He had seen
people moved by poems written in trenches, tacked to trees, passed hand-to-
hand amongst crowds, sung under fire. He had known people to live and die
in part by way of the meaning they gleaned from reading poems. But still there
were forces poems could not muster, powers poems could not defeat. Poetry
could be a force for change—it could alter consciousness, forge alliances, posi-
tion people differently within the culture—but it was rarely historically decisive
on its own. Oddly enough, a life given over explicitly to poetry's social mean-
ing forced him to interrogate the very idealism that came so easily to those
committed to the fantasy of poetry's transcendent self-sufficiency. Poetry, he
discovered, never had the effective autonomy of a true weapon. As always, the
limit case was his experience from 1937 to 1938. "If art is a weapon in the
thoughtless sense that many people think it is," he wrote in an unpublished
essay, "how could Republican Spain have lost?"

He had lived in Madrid in the days when it was the heart of the world. Now his own country, dominated by the inquisition, seemed to have no humanity. And his own heart was failing. In another notebook he records a dream of Spain: "In the dream, there was the battle on the hill, amazingly vivid and formal in its movements. And none of us escaped wounding. We were all maimed (men and women alike), but we consoled one another with our love, with the fullness of our love and pity." Now, "before the hyena's laugh gathers his bowels and tongue into knots, he remembers the days of his power and ease." Among the poems that follow, some come close to meeting the standard set by the notion that art can be a political weapon. Some, indeed, become chiseled, rhymed aggression, among them such brief unpublished poems as the following two quatrains, the first comparing the Supreme Court's roles in executing Sacco and Vanzetti in 1927 and Julius and Ethel Rosenberg in 1953:

June 19, 1953
This court, supreme in blindness and in hate,
supremely flaunts its lickspittle estate;
kills Jews today, as twenty-five years ago,
it killed Italians.

Pastoral—1954
Who used to lie with his love
   In the glade, far from the battle-sector,
   Now lies embraced by a lie-detector
And can not, dare not, move.

Striking because of the abrupt, elegantly brutal economy of their wit and their controlled rhythms and varied but deliberate rhymes, these poems are, if anything, even more unsettling for displaying Rolfe's craft in the service of a politically focused anger. In the context of the times, however, that articulate anger is itself a significant political accomplishment, for the cultural resources readily available for resistance are few indeed. "Living in 1951," he wrote in a note, "is like living in the peaks of the Andes—the air is thin and tense and we must develop new adaptations to survive."

You must write, he urged himself in a notebook, "as though you lived in an occupied country." For there was increasingly only one public culture in the country, a kind of bland conformity enforced at any human cost. He tried to warn his readers of what underlies the nation's self-congratulatory view of itself: "Friend, in your faith so like a marvelous loom," he wrote in June 1953 in the opening lines of an unpublished poem titled "A Double Hymn," "I hear the discord of a wheel of knives." By then, however, he was ill from a series of heart attacks. He had put together another book, titling it "Words and Ballads," but in the last year of his life he concentrated instead on a series of his strongest political poems, and some never made it into the plan for the book. Under pressure himself from HUAC, near the end of "A Double Hymn" he simply pleaded for relief:

> O friends and tyrants,
> O my ancestors, and you
> committee of the dead,
> judge me no more . . .

"My great crime," he told himself in one characterization of his Left politics, "is that I still believe in the perfectibility of human nature." But there was little audience then either for his ideals or his satiric critique. "Because it is prettier to protest an unrequited love than to protest the murder of a people," he wrote, "my poems are not popular in my own land."

Still, he persisted in performing acts of witness. Ten years after he returned from Spain he wrote and left unpublished one version of such an act of witness and remembrance, an unfinished poem to Federico García Lorca that we have placed second in the book. Part of the impulse behind these lines—the reference to the passage of time and the memory of García Lorca's poems in Spanish bookshops—ended up in "Elegia." But the passage as a whole has remained unpublished until now. Ten years had passed since the events he described, but describing them places him once again in his characteristic mode of testifying to lived history.

The time that passed had not taken the edge off the emotions he felt. If anything, he felt more strongly the need to make this moment part of the lyrical historical record. At no point in his life did Rolfe write what could be said to be a poetry that denies the passions of lived history. The only reason to write poems of that sort, perhaps, would be to urge inaction in the present, to spread the notion that proper historical understanding is possible only in retrospect. But Rolfe realized that even reflections on the past are written *in medias res;* thus all historically focused poetry becomes reflective advocacy and analysis for events in process, on the pain and ecstasy of historical experience as it is taking place. Yet it is never a question of simply transcribing experience, for there is no illusion here that language simply records and expresses. Rolfe was concerned instead with what difference language—poetic language—can make in a lived present. This is not, however, the open poetry of process we would have in the 1960s, for Rolfe is committed to writing finished poems and to making decisive political and moral judgments. One of the differences poetry can make, he realized, is to grant politically engaged analysis a certain formal and aesthetic resolution—and a claim on values that will have special power as a result. *Trees Became Torches,* published now, forty-one years after his death, gives us as eloquent an example as we could wish of a progressive poetry written in the midst of history, written on our behalf with our common history in view.

NOTES

1. Unless otherwise noted, all unpublished work by Rolfe is quoted from the Edwin Rolfe Archive in the Rare Books and Special Collections Library at the University of Illinois at Urbana-Champaign. The collection is in the process of being catalogued. Quotations from Rolfe's unpublished poetry and prose are © 1992 by Cary Nelson. *Trees Became Torches* includes about half of the poems in Rolfe's *Collected Poems,* published in 1993 by the University of Illinois Press. Readers may also consult Rolfe's *Collected Poems* for a detailed bibliography of Rolfe's publications in journals, newspapers, and anthologies, along with a listing of published reviews of each of his books. For an extended biographical essay on Rolfe, along with selected photographs and letters from his archive, see Cary Nelson and Jefferson Hendricks, eds., *Edwin Rolfe: A Biographical Essay and Guide to the Rolfe Archive at the University of Illinois at Urbana-Champaign* (Urbana: University of Illinois Library, 1990). Rolfe occasionally provided dates of composition with his published poems. We have supplied dates for additional poems whenever the information was available in his archive. Estimated dates of composition are based on the date of first publication.

2. Information about Rolfe's family comes from a series of interviews with Bern and Stanley Fishman (Rolfe's brothers), Mary Rolfe, and Leo Hurwitz, Rolfe's oldest friend.

3. When volunteers arrived in Spain they were asked a series of questions, including basic information such as their date of birth and home address, along with the nature and dates of their political affiliations. To the last question Rolfe answered "CP and YCL 1925." Rolfe was effectively noting that this was a distinction without a difference, though by the 1950s some people found it convenient to argue they never joined the Communist party but only the Young Communist League. Leonard Levenson, himself a Spanish Civil War veteran, supplied me with a 1939 microfilm copy of the answers Americans with some Party affiliation gave to the questions they were asked upon arriving at Albacete in Spain. Since then, I have

obtained a copy of Rolfe's entire International Brigades file from the Russian Center for the Preservation and Study of Documents of Recent History in Moscow. The file is in folder 975 of fund 545 in the Archive of the International Brigades of the Spanish Republican Army. It includes both a quite detailed questionnaire and a biographical summary that Rolfe filled out in Barcelona in 1938. In the latter he writes, "I joined the Young Communist League (then called the Young Workers' League) in 1924. In 1933 I was transferred to the Communist Party." John Gates suggested to me in an interview that young people who sought to join the Party were automatically assigned to the YCL. Rolfe, it should be noted, published two editorial cartoons in the *Daily Worker* in 1924.

4. Both Stanley Fishman and Leo Hurwitz independently recalled Rolfe's parents' political differences in interviews. Rolfe's International Brigades file makes this explicit. There he notes that both parents were early Party members, his mother since approximately 1923. Rolfe's father, however, was a Lovestoneite; i.e., he was part of the faction led by Jay Lovestone, which was collectively expelled from the Party in 1928. Rolfe's questionnaire gives the date of his father's expulsion as 1929. In any case, his parents separated not long after that. Rolfe wrote his father several times, urging him to leave the Lovestone group, which he did in 1933.

5. The files of the Experimental College at the University of Wisconsin at Madison are unusually complete. They include the written reports filed by Rolfe's advisors.

6. See Cary Nelson, *Repression and Recovery: Modern American Poetry and the Politics of Cultural Memory, 1910–1945* (Madison: University of Wisconsin Press, 1989), for a general discussion of 1930s poetry.

7. Rolfe's letters to Joseph Freeman are in the Joseph Freeman Archive at the Hoover Institution at Stanford University.

8. Interview with John Murra, Spanish Civil War veteran and later professor of anthropology at Cornell University.

9. Edwin Rolfe to Leo Hurwitz. Shortly before his death in 1991, Hurwitz kindly made Rolfe's letters to him available to us.

10. When Hemingway's piece "On the American Dead in Spain" was reprinted in *Somebody Had to Do Something: A Memorial to James Phillips Lardner* (Los Angeles: James Lardner Memorial Fund, 1939), the same Castelao print was selected to illustrate it.

11. Cf. Marilyn Rosenthal, *Poetry of the Spanish Civil War* (New York: New York University Press, 1975): "The image of Spain, of its cities, of its people, dying and destroyed, but becoming the seed of a new Spain, appears time and again among Hispanic poems. They regarded the war dead not as dead but as part of a living army, not as absent and finished but as sharing in the continuing struggle with the people with whom and for whom they had fought" (252).

12. Rolfe's note to Freeman is written on the backs of two copies of the memorial postcard the International Brigades issued to honor Arnold Reid. Since the postcards are undated and unstamped, they were presumably mailed in an envelope. The Freeman Archive at the Hoover Institution is not yet catalogued, but the postcards are in a temporary file labeled "Arnold Reid."

13. Interview with Thomas Viertel, July 30, 1991. The best history of HUAC's impact on Hollywood is Larry Ceplair and Steven Englund, *The Inquisition in Hollywood: Politics in the Film Community, 1930–1960* (Berkeley: University of California Press, 1983). For a wider history see David Caute, *The Great Fear: The Anti-Communist Purge under Truman and Eisenhower* (New York: Simon and Schuster, 1978).

14. Edward Dmytryk broke with the Ten and testified before HUAC in 1951, naming twenty-six names in public testimony. He also recanted his earlier Left commitments in a *Saturday Evening Post* article, which Albert Maltz answered in his "Open Letter to the *Saturday Evening Post* on Edward Dmytryk," published in the *Hollywood Reporter* in 1951.

15. Karen Ford, "First Love," paper presented at a symposium on Edwin Rolfe, University of Illinois, October 1990.

16. Rolfe describes how and why he was fired in a letter to Leo Hurwitz. Mary Rolfe confirmed in an interview that "Definition" was based on that experience.

17. A number of Rolfe's friends and family members, including Mary Rolfe, volunteered the information that "Ballad of the Noble Intentions" was written in response to hearing that Odets had testified before HUAC.

18. Ford, "First Love."

19. Sheean himself wrote a poem about the incident titled "Puigcerdá," published in the October 4, 1938, issue of *New Masses* and in the 1938 anthology *Salud!: Poems, Stories, and Sketches of Spain by American Writers*, ed. Alan Calmer (New York: International Publishers), 41. Sheean's poem also ends with the image of the swan:

> But the swan there,
> the swan upon the water—
> the swan's enchantment over the silver water—
> moves still,
> pure and proud,
> disdains the shrapnel,
> scorns the thunder.
>
> The swan in beauty floats upon the lake,
> serene before the choice that death must make.

See also the last line of Miguel Hernández's famous Spanish Civil War romance "The Winds of the People," *Poems for Spain* (1939):

> for there are nightingales that sing
> above the rifles' voice
> and in the battles' mist.

20. See *The Lincoln Battalion* (New York: Random House, 1939) for Rolfe's own experience of Segura de los Baños.

21. Born in Malaga in 1905, Manuel Altolaguirre was a cofounder of the influential prewar magazine *Litoral*. He also started *Poesia* in Paris and *1616* in London and was a cofounder of *Hora de España* (Spain's Hour), one of the major antifascist literary magazines of the Spanish Civil War. His book *La lenta libertad* was awarded the Premio Nacional de Literatura in 1933. In exile in Mexico he became a filmmaker. He died in a car crash on his first return to Spain in 1959.

22. Hemingway's letter is published in its entirety in Nelson and Hendricks, *Edwin Rolfe*.

23. A much shorter version of the story appeared in the *Los Angeles Times*. Rolfe saved both clippings.

The Spanish Civil War

First Love

Again I am summoned to the eternal field
green with the blood still fresh at the roots of flowers,
green through the dust-rimmed memory of faces
that moved among the trees there for the last time
before the final shock, the glazed eye, the hasty mound.

But why are my thoughts in another country?
Why do I always return to the sunken road through corroded hills,
with the Moorish castle's shadow casting ruins over my shoulder
and the black-smocked girl approaching, her hands laden with grapes?

I am eager to enter it, eager to end it.
Perhaps this one will be the last one.
And men afterward will study our arms in museums
and nod their heads, and frown, and name the inadequate dates
and stumble with infant tongues over the strange place-names.

But my heart is forever captive of that other war
that taught me first the meaning of peace and of comradeship

and always I think of my friend who amid the apparition of bombs
saw on the lyric lake the single perfect swan.

1943

THE SPANISH CIVIL WAR

A Federico García Lorca

Ten years have passed since I found in a book shop
        in Albacete,
The paper-bound case of jewels which I treasure still, the
        book *Romancero Gitano,*
And turned to the first poem, the "Romance de la Luna,
        Luna,"
And read and found fabulous peace in the midst of the war.

Later, in Madrid, the lads of the guerrilleros
Crossed the midnight lines from madness to the light of
        the Casa de Alianza.
And told us (Langston was there, and Rafael, and María
        Teresa)
That they came from the choked south, from your buried
        city, Granada.

And they told how they met in the streets the people who
        told them in whispers
Of the way you died, with surprise in your eyes,
        as you recognized your assassins,
The men with the patent-leather hats and souls of patent-leather.

c. 1948

Epitaph

FOR ARNOLD REID
D. JULY 27, 1938
AT VILLALBA DE LOS ARCOS

Deep in this earth,
deeper than grave was dug
ever, or body of man ever lowered,
runs my friend's blood,
spilled here. We buried him
here where he fell,
here where the sniper's eye
pinned him, and everything
in a simple moment's
quick explosion of pain was over.

Seven feet by three
measured the trench we dug,
ample for body of man ever murdered.
Now in this earth his blood
spreads through far crevices,
limitless, nourishing vineyards for miles around,
olive groves slanted on hillocks, trees
green with young almonds, purple with ripe figs,
and fields no enemy's boots
can ever desecrate.

This is no grave,
no, nor a resting place.
This is the plot where the self-growing seed
sends its fresh fingers to turn soil aside,
over and under earth ceaselessly growing,
over and under earth endlessly growing.

July 30, 1938
Villalba de los Arcos

Death by Water

On May 30 1937 the small Spanish coastal steam-
ship *Ciudad de Barcelona* was torpedoed and sunk
off the coast of Malgrat by a submarine which
the Non-Intervention Committee preferred to de-
signate as "of unknown nationality." More than
a hundred volunteers, twelve of them Americans,
perished.

Nearing land, we heard the cry of gulls and
saw their shadows in sunlight on the topmost deck,
or coasting unconcerned on each wavecrest, they rested
after their scavenging, scudding the ship's length.

And we thought of the albatross—an old man going crazy,
his world an immenseness of water, none of it to drink;
and the vultures descending on an Ethiopian plain:
all of us were the living corpse, powerless, bleeding.

And suddenly the shock. We felt the boat shiver.
I turned to Oliver, saw his eyes widen,
stare past the high rails, waiting, waiting . . .
Others stumbled past us. And suddenly the explosion.

Men in twenty languages cried out to comrades
as the blast tore the ship, and the water, like lava,
plunged through the hull, crushing metal and flesh before it,
splintering cabins, the sleepers caught unconscious.

Belted, we searched for companions but lost them
in turmoil of faces; swept toward the lifeboats
and saw it was useless. Too many were crowding them.
Oliver dived. I followed him, praying.

In the water the sea-swell hid for a moment
Oliver swimming, strongly, away from me.
Then his voice, calmly: "Here, keep his head above."
We helped save a drowning man, kept him afloat until

dories approached. Looking backward, we saw
the prow high in air, and Carlos, unconcerned,
throwing fresh belts to the tiring swimmers.
Steam, flame crept toward him, but he remained absorbed . . .

2

On shore, later, a hundred of us gone,
we are too weak to weep for them, to listen to
consoling words. We are too tired
to return the grave smiles of the rescuing people.
Too drained. Sorrow can never be the word.

But beyond the numbness the vivid faces
of comrades burn in our brains: their songs
in quiet French villages, their American laughter
tug at responding muscles in our lips,
shout against ears that have heard their voices living.

Fingers, convulsive, form fists. Teeth
grate now, audibly. We stifle curses,
thought but unuttered. While many grieve,
their hands reach outward, fingers extended—
the image automatic—ready for rifles

until night brings us sleep, and dreams
of violent death by drowning, dreams
of journey, slow advances through vineyards,
seeking cover in wheatfields, finding always
the fascist face behind the olive tree.

August 1937
Madrid

City of Anguish

FOR MILTON WOLFF

At midnight they roused us. In the distance we heard
verberations of thunder. "To the cellar," they ordered.
"It's safest under the stairway." Pointing,
a veteran led us. The children, whimpering,
followed the silent women who would never
sing again strolling in the *Paseo* on Sunday evenings.
In the candle-light their faces were granite.

"Artillery," muttered Enrico, cursing.
Together we turned at the lowest stair.
"Come on," he said. "It's better on the rooftop.
More fireworks, better view." Slowly we ascended
past the stalled lift, felt through the roof door,
squinted in moonless darkness.

We counted the flashes, divided the horizon,
90 degrees for Enrico, 90 for me.
"Four?" "No, five!" We spotted the big guns when
the sounds came crashing, split-seconds after light.
Felt the slight earthquake tremor when shells fell
square on the Gran Via; heard high above our heads
the masculine shriek of the shell descending—
the single sharp rifle-crack, the inevitable dogs
barking, angry, roused from midsummer sleep.
The lulls grew fewer: soon talking subsided
as the cannonade quickened. Each flash in darkness
created horizon, outlined huge buildings.
Off a few blocks to the north, the *Telefónica*
reared its massive shoulders, its great symbol profile
in dignity, like the statue of Moses pointing,
agèd but ageless, to the Promised Land.

2

Deafening now, the sky is aflame with
unnatural lightning. The ear—

like the scout's on patrol—gauges each explosion.
The mind—neither ear nor eye is aware of it—
calculates destruction, paints the dark pictures
of beams fallen, ribs crushed beneath them; beds
blown with their innocent sleepers to agonized
death.
        And the great gaping craters in streets
yawn, hypnotic to the terrified madman,
sane a mere hour ago.
                The headless body
stands strangely, totters for a second, falls.
The girl speeds screaming through wreckage; her
        hair is
wilder than torture.
              The solitary foot,
deep-arched, is perfect on the cobbles, naked,
strong, ridged with strong veins, upright, complete . . .

The city weeps. The city shudders, weeping.

The city weeps: for the moment is silent—
the pause in the idiot's symphony, prolonged
beyond the awaited crashing of cymbals, but
the hands are in mid-air, the instruments gleaming:
the swastika'd baton falls! and the clatter of
thunder begins again.
            Enrico beckons me.
Fires there. Where? Toward the *Casa de Campo*.
And closer. There. The *Puerta del Sol* exudes
submarine glow in the darkness, alive with
strange twisting shapes, skyfish of stars,
fireworks of death, mangled lives, silent lips.
In thousands of beds now the muscles of men are
aroused, flexed for springing, quivering, tense,
that moments ago were relaxed, asleep.

3

It is too late for sleep now.
Few hours are left before dawn. We wait for
the sun's coming . . . And it rises, sulphurous
through smoke. It is too late for sleep.

The city weeps. The city wakens, weeping.

And the Madrileños rise from wreckage, emerge
from shattered doorways . . .
                              But always the wanderer,
the old woman searching, digging among debris.
In the morning light her crazed face is granite.

And the beggar sings among the ruins:

    All night, all night
    flared in my city the bright
    cruel explosion of bombs.
    All night, all night,
    there, where the soil and stone
    spilled like brains from the sandbag's head,
    the bodiless head lay staring;
    while the anti-aircraft barked,
    barked at the droning plane,
    and the dogs of war, awakened,
    howled at the hidden moon.
    And a star fell, omen of ill,
    and a man fell, lifeless,
    and my wife fell, childless,
    and, friendless, my friend.
    And I stumbled away from them, crying
    from eyeless lids, blinded.
    Trees became torches
    lighting the avenues
    where lovers huddled in terror
    who would be lovers no longer.

All night, all night
flared in my city the bright
cruel explosion of hope—
all night
all night . . .

4

Come for a joyride in Madrid: the August morning
is cleared of smoke and cloud now; the journalists
dip their hard bread in the *Florida* coffee,
no longer distasteful after sour waking.
Listen to Ryan, fresh from the lines, talking
    (Behind you the memory of bombs beats
    the blood in the brain's vessels—the dream broken,
    sleep pounded to bits by the unending roar of
    shells in air, the silvery bombs descending,
    rabid spit of machine guns and the carnival flare
    of fire in the sky):
                        "Why is it, why?
when I'm here in the trenches, half-sunk in mud,
blanket drenched, hungry, I dream of Dublin,
of home, of the girls? But give me a safe spot,
clean linen, bed and all, sleep becomes nightmare
of shrapnel hurtling, bombs falling, the screaming of bullets,
their thud on the brain's parapet. Why? Why?"

Exit the hotel. The morning constitutional.
Stroll down the avenues. Did Alfonso's car
detour past barricades? Did broken mains splatter him?
Here's the bellyless building; four walls, no guts.
But the biggest disaster's the wrecking of power:
thirty-six hours and no power: electric
sources are severed. The printer is frantic:
how print the leaflet, the poster, or set
the type for the bulletin?
                        After his food
a soldier needs cigarettes, something to read,
something to think about: words to pull

the war-weary brain back to life from forgetfulness:
spirited words, the gestures of Dolores,
majestic Pasionaria speaking—
mother to men, mother of revolutions,
winner of battles, comforter of defenders;
her figure magnificent as any monument
constructed for heroes; her voice a symphony,
consoling, urging, declaiming in prophecy,
her forehead the wide plateaus of her country,
her eyes constant witness of her words' truth.

5

Needless to catalogue heroes. No man
weighted with rifle, digging with nails in earth,
quickens at the name. Hero's a word for
peacetime. Battle
knows only three realities: enemy, rifle, life.

No man knows war or its meaning who has not
stumbled from tree to tree, desperate for cover,
or dug his face deep in earth, felt the ground pulse with
the ear-breaking fall of death. No man knows war
who never has crouched in his foxhole, hearing
the bullets an inch from his head, nor the zoom of
planes like a Ferris wheel strafing the trenches . . .

War is your comrade struck dead beside you,
his shared cigarette still alive in your lips.

1937
Madrid

Casualty

It seemed
the sky was a harbor, into which rode
black iron cruisers, silently, their guns
poised like tiger-heads on turret-haunches.

It seemed the sky was an olive grove, ghostly
in moonlight, and Very-light, with deadly crossfire
splitting it, proving a new theorem with rifles,
unknown in any recalled geometry.

And then he woke, choking. Saw sky as sky
in purest moonlight; and the searchlight beams paled
against it, and he heard Tibidábo's guns
burst against space. Then one bomb, shrieking,

found the thin axis of his whirling fears,
the exact center.

March 17, 1938
Barcelona

About Eyes

The terror of the serene plane is in their eyes:
look deeply, see the wings dip, and the revolving nose

split sky and cloud, ten thousand feet above
the remembered city of women with violent hearts,

incredibly aged children, dark-eyed, who recall
the propeller's sound and the panic
from the days of the womb's darkness.

The eyes contain, reflect more than the image photographed
in the almanacs, the newspapers, the albums airmen are fond of.

The joy of the plunge through mist into sun is unknown to
the wide anonymous eyes of the dwellers in bombed cities.

The eyes reveal everything: the inhuman grace
of the silver flight, and the first melodic hum,
deceitful, cruel, of the synchronized guns and motors

and the arc-plummet fall of the bombs, the grotesque explosion,
the hysteria of the insane siren, the last deception.

Eyes of a Blind Man

FOR COMMANDANTE FORT OF THE FRANCO-BELGE
BATTALION OF THE FOURTEENTH (INTERNATIONAL)
BRIGADE, WHO STARED AT A WOMAN IN THE CASA
DE REPOSA DE GENERAL LUCASZ, IN MADRID,
IN THE LATE AUTUMN OF 1937.

Her voice is a magnet into which flows
all I remember. It is her voice I see.
Not her mythical eyes alive with reflections
nor her moon-lucent throat nor the way her head's poised
proudly above it; nor the luxuriant hair
flowing backward from temples like grass from a lake's shore;
no, nor the nose and its breathing nostrils.
Neither mouth nor lips nor the vivid teeth
do I see, nor her finely-lobed ears.
Her voice is all that's visible to me.

By her voice I note her coming and her going,
engrave her movements as a beach records
continual change of tides. All that remains now
is the memory of sight, like a special statue
seen in a childhood museum. The rest
is sorrow to sense, strong wine to smell,
anguish to possess, even in the mind's eye.

But her voice remains, palpable, lucid, real.
Her voice is now what her eyes and the curve of her lips are
to all other men.

September 7, 1937
Madrid

Elegy for Our Dead

There is a place where, wisdom won, right recorded,
men move beautifully, striding across fields
whose wheat, wind-marshalled, wanders unguarded
in unprotected places; where earth, revived, folds
all growing things closely to itself: the groves
of bursting olives, the vineyards ripe and heavy with
glowing grapes, the oranges like million suns; and graves
where lie, nurturing all these fields, my friends in death.

With them, deep in coolness, are memories of France and
the exact fields of Belgium, midnight marches in snows—
the single-file caravan high in the Pyrenees: the land
of Spain unfolded before them, dazzling the young Balboas.
This earth is enriched with Atlantic salt, spraying
the live, squinting eyelids, even now, of companions—
with towns of America, towers and mills, sun playing
always, in stone streets, wide fields—all men's dominions.

Honor for them in this lies: that theirs is no special
strange plot of alien earth. Men of all lands here
lie side by side, at peace now after the crucial
torture of combat, bullet and bayonet gone, fear
conquered forever. Yes, knowing it well, they were willing
despite it to clothe their vision with flesh. And their rewards,
not sought for self, live in new faces, smiling,
remembering what they did here. Deeds were their last words.

September 20, 1937
Madrid

Postscript to a War

FOR MICHAEL GORDON

We must remember cleanly why we fought,
clearly why we left these inadequate shores
and turned our eyes, hearts, Spainward. We must never
lie to ourselves again, deceive ourselves with dreams
that make sleep sluggish. Our world
is new now, clean and clear: our eyes can see
the perfect bone and tissue now, remembering
the flesh cut open, the gangrened limbs, the rot
that almost, almost . . . but did not reach the heart.

And if we find all known things changed
now, after two years amid fabulous truth;
if we find dulled the once sharp edges
of trivial loves; even if we find
our truest loves indifferent, even false—
we must remember cleanly why we went,
clearly why we fought; and returning, see
with truth's unfilmed eye what remains constant,
the loyalties which endure, the loves that grow,
the certainties men need, live for, die to build,
the certainties that make all living tolerable.

February 24, 1939

Brigadas Internacionales

To say *We were right* is not boastful,
nor *We saw, when all others were blind*
nor *We acted, while others ignored or uselessly wept.*

We have the right to say this
because in purest truth it is also recorded:
We died, while others in cowardice looked on.

Just as the man is false who never says *I*
nor asserts his own deeds in pride, or disclaims his wrongs,
so too would we be less than truly what we are

if we did not now, to all the embattled world,
proclaim in pride: *We saw. We acted. Fought.*
We died, while others in cowardice lived on.

November 1939

Paris—Christmas 1938

You will remember, when the bombs
invade your softest midnight dream,
when terror flowing through your limbs
brings madness to your vulnerable room;

you will remember, when you stare at walls
familiar, patterned in a memorized
design, and watch the plaster as it falls,
abrupt, concussive—and you shrink back dazed

and all your body, that a moment past
was quiet, relaxed upon the comforting bed,
will stiffen, flex in fear; a host
of insane images will bring the dead

of many cities back to life again:
the dead you pleasantly ignored, and hid
from self and others; you will clutch the lone
solace of men who soon too will be dead

and count your sins, and know that they were crimes,
and curse your quiet, and respect, at last, these dead;
yes, you will remember—when the initial bombs
insanely fall into *your* life—Madrid.

Dec., 1938–July, 1939
Paris—New York

Elegia

Madrid   Madrid   Madrid   Madrid
I call your name endlessly, savor it like a lover.
Ten irretrievable years have exploded like bombs
since last I saw you, since last I slept
in your arms of tenderness and wounded granite.
Ten years since I touched your face in the sun,
ten years since the homeless Guadarrama winds
moaned like shivering orphans through your veins
and I moaned with them.
                          When I think of you, Madrid,
locked in the bordello of the Universal Pimp,
the blood that rushes to my heart and head
blinds me, and I could strangle your blood-bespattered jailors,
choke them with these two hands which once embraced you.
When I think of your breathing body of vibrancy and sun,
silently I weep, in my own native land
which I love no less because I love you more.
Yet I know, in the heart of my heart, that until your liberation
rings through the world of free men near and far
I must wander like an alien everywhere.

Madrid, in these days of our planet's anguish,
forged by the men whose mock morality
begins and ends with the tape of the stock exchanges,
I too sometimes despair. I weep with your dead young poet.
Like him I curse our age and cite the endless wars,
the exiles, dangers, fears, our weariness
of blood, and blind survival, when so many
homes, wives, even memories, are lost.

Yes, I weep with Garcilaso. I remember
your grave face and your subtle smile
and the heart-leaping beauty of your daughters and even
the tattered elegance of your poorest sons.
I remember the gaiety of your *milicianos*—
my comrades-in-arms. What other city
in history ever raised a battalion of barbers
or reared its own young shirt-sleeved generals?

And I recall them all. If I ever forget you,
Madrid, Madrid, may my right hand lose its cunning.

I speak to you, Madrid, as lover, husband, son.
Accept this human trinity of passion.
I love you, therefore I am faithful to you
and because to forget you would be to forget
everything I love and value in the world.
Who is not true to you is false to every man
and he to whom your name means nothing never loved
and they who would use your flesh and blood again
as a whore for their wars and their wise investments,
may they be doubly damned! the double murderers
of you and their professed but fictional honor,
of everything untarnished in our time.

Wandering, bitter, in this bitter age,
I dream of your broad avenues like brooks in summer
with your loveliest children alive in them like trout.
In my memory I walk the Calle de Velasquez
to the green Retiro and its green gardens.
Sometimes when I pace the streets of my own city
I am transported to the flowing Alcalá
and my footsteps quicken, I hasten to the spot
where all your living streams meet the Gateway to the Sun.
Sometimes I brood in the shadowed Plaza Mayor
with the ghosts of old Kings and Inquisitors
agitating the balconies with their idiot stares
(which Goya later knew) and under whose stone arches,
those somber rooms beneath the colonnades,
the old watchmaker dreams of tiny, intricate minutes,
the old woman sells pencils and gaudy amber combs,
dreaming of the days when her own body was young,
and the rheumatic peasant with fingers gnarled as grapevines
eagerly displays his muscat raisins;
and the intense boys of ten, with smouldering aged eyes,
kneel, and gravely, quixotically,
polish the rawhide boots of the soldiers in for an hour

from the mined trenches of the Casa de Campo,
from their posts, buzzing with death, within the skeleton
of University City.
                    And the girls stroll by,
the young ones, conscious of their womanhood,
and I hear in my undying heart called Madrid
the soldiers boldly calling to them: Oye, guapa, oye!

I remember your bookshops, the windows always crowded
with new editions of the Gypsy Ballads,
with *Poetas en la España Leal*
and *Romanceros de los Soldados en las Trincheras.*
There was never enough food, but always poetry.
Ah the flood of song that gushed with your blood
into the world during your three years of glory!

And I think: it is a fine thing to be a man
only when man has dignity and manhood.
It is a fine thing to be proud and fearless
only when pride and courage have direction, meaning.
And in our world no prouder words were spoken
in those three agonized years than *I am from Madrid.*

Now ten years have passed with small explosions of hope,
yet you remain, Madrid, the conscience of our lives.
So long as you endure, in chains, in sorrow,
I am not free, no one of us is free.
Any man in the world who does not love Madrid
as he loves a woman, as he values his sex,
that man is less than a man and dangerous,
and so long as he directs the affairs of our world
I must be his undying enemy.

Madrid   Madrid   Madrid   Madrid
Waking and sleeping, your name sings in my heart
and your need fills all my thoughts and acts
(which are gentle but have also been intimate with rifles).
Forgive me, I cannot love you properly from afar—

no distant thing is ever truly loved—
but this, in the wrathful impotence of distance,
I promise: Madrid, if I ever forget you,
may my right hand lose its human cunning,
may my arms and legs wither in their sockets,
may my body be drained of its juices and my brain
go soft and senseless as an imbecile's.
And if I die before I can return to you,
or you, in fullest freedom, are restored to us,
my sons will love you as their father did
Madrid   Madrid   Madrid

November 6, 1948

Portraits

Manuela

Lovelier than the river in the spring
Manuela walks, her body flowing by . . .

Ageless she is, and cageless: she is only
music and sky, flowers and wine, the deep
feel of dark shimmering water at my thigh.

Her face at midnight is all life; at dawn
the sunlight makes a prison of her hair,
her brow, her throat, and all that's hidden; then
I enter her, an eager prisoner.

The convict of the night returns to her.

I could lie still in wonder at her side
but her breathing and the wind that stirs her hair
make my hands jealous, restless, and my body
loses its calm, and I must waken her.

After the storm Manuela sleeps again.
Her body is a haven and a fire,
lovely as autumn on the nearby hills.

I have no need of her now: she is only
music and bread, flowers and earth, the dark
feel of deep murmuring water at my thigh.

Lovelier than the river in the fall
Manuela walks, her body flowing by . . .

Eyes of a Boy

FOR HILARIO, who stared like this at his divisional commander, Valentín González, before he was killed at the age of fifteen on a hill near Venta de Campesinos in September 1938.

There is greatness in you, greater than your shoulders
sturdier than a grown tree. There is warmth which my father,
my own father, never had. I like to look at your eyes,
brown, warm, sometimes soft as a woman's,
soft as my mother's, or your heavy-lobed ears
catching each sound in air, whether of rearguard traitor
or enemy boast, whether of plane flying
or bullet whistling or shell shuddering by.

And your beard, your black beard, Barbas! Your face
now arrogant, now soft, now laughing with
a special laughter. There is always a joke being
whispered in your ear, which you never keep to yourself;
the whole world must hear it and share in your mirth.
And your teeth, small and even, now sharp and clean with
the last lusty meal; and your wide mouth moving,
the heavy lips humorous, smiling at your men,
your two young commanders, Merino and Policarpo—
whom you call *My sons*—talking with companions.

It is painful, sometimes, to be young, small, a boy.
I am impatient to grow, to become a man,
big enough to lug the rifle of your faith,
old enough to march alongside you, Campesino,
to be with you in battle. Yet even now, I think,
I'm old enough.

August 25, 1937
Alaládes Henares
Dedication added: 1938

PORTRAITS

The Melancholy Comus

FOR CHARLES CHAPLIN

1

Look closely: from nowhere he leaps into the screen
and fills it with light and with luminous joy
and shadow of authentic mystery.
He smiles, but the eyes are haunted. Or the eyes
glimmer with laughter, but the lips tremble.
He moves, and we see a man move. Look again:
it's a woman walking with the grace of women.
And still another time: a child smiles from the screen.
Yet nothing clashes; man, woman, child are one,
natural variant aspects of the selfsame image.
Grace is there, and the generous sex, and strong
decisive gestures, and hurt, and the helpless exposed
face of the child, desiring love, a smile,
eager for approbation, quick to perceive the frown,
the hidden annoyance, the unsaid words "I don't want you."

But over all, as we watch from the darkened hall,
we feel the toughness, we know the tenderness,
we sense the great love and the mastery.
In him, blended perfectly, are man, woman, child:
that synthesis so few attain,
that delights us, pleasures us to come upon
but would in our own selves, indeed, embarrass us.

2

Mimic of the small dry crumbs of our joy
and the inedible shoestrings of our indignation
and the hurled pie of outrage and of hurt
and the sudden soul-washing sight of the lovely girl,
he mirrors the true motions of our regimented lives,
our nerve-ends, our goose-stepping muscles. And he sings
our unwavering happiness and unchanging sorrows
and our loneliness from which there is no escape.

3

Because he is what we would be
we love him. Since we cannot love ourselves,
knowing too well the blemishes that mar
our lives, our loves,

our rich, inhibited love
encompasses his image on the screen:
our brains think his thoughts,
our hands feel what he feels,
our own feet ache in his comic shoes.

4

The brain has arrows,
the mouth has swords,
but the body, fluid and flowing, is all music.

Even in prison,
exposed, alone,
he builds the vaulting towers of the inner castle.

The eyes have malice,
the ears have chains,
but the hands are winged like the fingers of a pianist.

Surrounded, held at bay
by policmen of the mind,
his faith is tethered subtly to tomorrow's sunrise.

The heart has miracles.

The soul has wings.

5

Slowly the walls of the world's room press inward
as in a penny-dreadful or a Kafka dream,
and the naked whimpering Soul and Ego, unprotected,
shrink and clutch each other in a bleak embrace,

loveless, awaiting extinction, pleading "Faster, faster!"
but the walls move slowly in their mechanical grooves,
gently, unhurried; and the terrified, fleshless lovers
watch them, the maniac's shriek locked in their frozen throats.

And I look: my body, with all its frailties and fears,
inhabits the skin and bones of both; my body
recoils from the doom that looms closer as mountains of ice
closed down, long ago, on a green and younger earth.
But I turn my eyes away, thinking "I do not see it,
and what I do not see does not exist,"
and I conjure pleasanter visions in which the world
is not converging wall but ever-expanding heaven.

But sometimes my imagination fails me.
Sometimes I cannot help but see what is real
and menacing and hateful as any chamber of horrors
glimpsed by a child on a Sunday museum-tour.
Sometimes I despair: I feel as the suicide feels
the moment before he pulls the innocent trigger or tests
the chair he stands on before he kicks it away or lets
the razor's edge leap toward the vibrant vein.

And in anger I cry to those who will listen:
What kind of world is this where he who speaks of man,
and man's sorrows, and man's deep longings,
and man's unmitigated loneliness,
is looked on as a leper? And he who speaks of love
is laughed at, reviled, showered with steel and filth?
While those whom we are taught to listen and look up to
say *peace* as if it were a foul word.

1948

Essay on Dreiser (1871–1945)

Death underlines our loss. The man who moved
mountains of men is dead on a mountain peak.
And those he hated, those whom he always loved
are quiet now: we will not hear him speak,
flushed, impulsive, angry again. He never
truly achieved old age despite his years;
never evaded combat, rarely ran for cover;
in his eighth decade undertook new chores,
left jumbled notes to plague the stunned survivor.

Whether we care or not, we are his heirs
and ours the busybody task is: to decipher
the massive marginalia of his plodding years,
the words piled high on words, the flowing river
of novels, polemics, poems, apologies.
No matter where we turn, we will be bogged
deep in a brooding delta of discrepancies,
in work diffused too widely to be catalogued,
a life too intricate for neat obituaries.

And questions still confound us: why,
more than ten years ago, in the illiterate south,
caught in the compulsive human act, did he deny
the very power that gave his novels worth—
his own virility? And he, who profoundly knew
what casts the malignant mote in mankind's eye,
why did he gibe the English, bait the Jew?
To say he typified the world's protracted youth
is true but does not tell the essential truth.

His foibles were not his alone. Voltaire
in another century and to a like degree
debased his precious coinage in the fire
of similar falsehoods; and even in our day
men who lead nations through blood, sweat, tears,
adding immortal moments to our history,
at other moments mouth the ugly lie
that quickens hatreds and prolongs for years
the myths that send men brutally to kill, to die.

But now he is home, he is safe. No more
will he dig in the lower depths of our despair
nor engage in public boxing matches nor
praise motherhood, damn poverty and laissez faire.
His death embarrassed us: in the city where he died
no liberal journal dared identify the spade,
to call him what he was, a communist.
To do so would have pricked the provincial pride
which now will label him our foremost novelist.

His death still leaves the major question-mark
unanswered: how a man of vast confusions,
of usual failings, reflecting all the dark
complexities of our ignorance and passions,
can yet create a life in life, illumine
those crevices we others shrink from, and explore
the tortuous highways of the soul, the human
heart and its tempestuous truths—the core
of our most devious motives in eternal war.

But speculation serves no purpose. Dreiser
was what he was. No judgment is complete.
Much as we wish he had been surer, wiser,
we cannot change the fact. The man was great
in a way Americans uniquely understand
who know the uneven contours of their land,
its storms, its droughts, its huge and turbulent
Mississippi, where his youth was spent,
whose floods entomb its truest sons in the ocean's sand.

December 29, 1945

Vincent

The Borinage receded, at last, like a bad dream
although he strained to retain it in his vision.
Like sodden sand, dark and weighted like leaden
reluctance, he watched it slip through the sieve of his hand
and memory; until at length all that remained
was the somber cottage in the somber region,
the room illumined darkly, and the workmen,
with faces smudged by the cold stuff of fire,
eating their sodden roots at the end of a bleak day.

Later, much later, the damp still deep in him,
eating away at the arteries of his burdened brain,
he saw, for the first time, sunlight. And was dazed,
then dazzled out of his darkness. Child of the cold fog,
he fell in love with light, saw how it foamed
in specks and dots and whorls and hurricanes
of brilliant hysteria; and his burning brush
cut fiercely through the cold traditional palette,
exploding into pigment more radiant than sun.

Then, toward the end, mixed madness and self-murder,
killed cold, and coddled forms, killed ways of seeing
object as object. Turned wheatfields into seas,
flowers to forests, faces into fields
of constant, bitter combat; and a small room
into a history more true than any book.

Finally, defeated as all are finally defeated,
severed and sent off the famous ear, preparing
a small symbolic grave prophetic of the last one.

Called, weaker every moment, for help, help!
But no one heard except a penniless brother.
And no help came. What could he do but die
who saw the blazing truth denied, the lie
of coldness wooed, praised in salons, enshrined?

Went down at last. And those—how few—who mourned,
mourned a mad and victorious man,
an undefeated eye.

Nuthin but Brass

FOR CAB CALLOWAY

"Please, Mr. Orchestra, play us another tune."

Let the old broken hag die on the street:
the D.S.C. will haul the hulk away,
clean up the mess. Let the dinkey rattle
under the El all night all day:
nobody'll notice. The sky will go
purple or red or cloudy over us—
My St. Louis Woman and *Minnie the Moocher*
will sprinkle the star dust and cover us.

*   *   *

The last magenta light is dimmed in the dome,
the Academy heaven goes black as any night
save for the spotlight tinkling the glass
of the imitation crystal chandelier.

Music floats up from the pit, or maybe
the pipes in the wall are grinding through the hall.
The pink-and-gold curtain rises like an angel,
the balcony lights an enormous cigaret

an there aint nuthin left in the hall but brass:
three saxophones, three cornets, a huge bass drum,
a lone bass viol—and cigaret smoke
weaving metallic patterns in the spotlight.

He is a reed walking out on the stage
with a thinner reed in his hand. Each body
strains forward in its seat, each body sways
before his body answers to the low moan swoon

swooping down through him from the balcony,
from Harlem round the corner, from 14th Street,
from Soho and gaslit left bank rooms,
from bodies sensed in beds in a million rooms . . .

O the brass is alive, his voice is brass!
his voice is a drum and a flute and a low
silvery saxophone zooming in the night,
his body a cushion for all love and lust.

A million Minnies dreaming of the King of Sweden,
(wishing you were dead, you bastard, YOU!)
counting a million dollars in nickels and dimes
a million, billion, quadrillion times!

Baby, the world grows smaller than a rose
(smaller than a room, a single bed
where two warm bodies with space to spare
are attenuated reeds of reciprocal play).

Baby, the world aint a thing to us now
and we doan need no gin an no cigarets
an no spot on a dancefloor smaller than a dime
to congeal you and me in the bumps, baby.

All of it is true. No promissory note
is needed to insure the reality of dreaming,
the wail and the moaning, the break in the voice:
"Will you take this man?" "I do, I do!"
The song is wilder now, his voice is drowned
in waves of muscatel wine from the mouths
of the muted cornets and the derbied saxophones
and the pianist jigging on the keyboard.

They all suddenly rise and discard the derbies.
Awake, you little dreaming fools in the dome!
This is no wine. It's synthetic gin,
it's rasping tobacco, it's fragmentary love

and lust; and the voice you surrendered to
is now but a grinning mouth, and the cool
clean million is spent, you profligates!
and there aint nuthin left in the hall but brass.

Curtain. He's still grinning, but the smile
sags at the corners, at its soft beginning.
Put on your coats. The Academy splurges
a last time in light before it goes to sleep.

June 1932

Work and Revolution

Catalogue of I

When I write I am no longer I alone
but more, much more. Male? American? Yes.
Solely and purely of this century? True,
but insufficient, inexact. I am the arm too
tearing from Paris street the paving stone,
the voice, two centuries old, shouting *Aux barricades!*
the Alicante orphan, the widow in Madrid,
the stunned revived survivor of Stalingrad,
the cotton-clad exile in the caves of loess,
the pueblo-dweller in dry and dying Taos.
And more: I am the pilgrim of every race,
of every age, landing on every shore:
he of the slant eyes, blond hair, black face,
and the galley-slave who fainted on his oar,
and those who die in fields, mines, factories,
more numerous than those who fall in war.
Yet I am he as well: the soldier, the recruit,
he who fights, falls, runs, wins, dies,
and fights again. Not he who causes war
or welcomes, profits by it. I am the everywhere
everyman of the thousand tongues and eyes
and billion always dying deathless brothers.

Who fears inclusion in this catalogue of I
is useless, valueless, deserves to die.
Yet he, my doomed and unloved brother,
is also I, is also I.

November 24, 1948

Asbestos

Knowing (as John did) nothing of the way
men act when men are roused from lethargy,
and having nothing (as John had) to say
to those he saw were starving just as he

starved, John was like a workhorse. Day by day
he saw his sweat cement the granite tower
(the edifice his bone had built), to stay
listless as ever, older every hour.

John's deathbed is a curious affair:
the posts are made of bone, the spring of nerves,
the mattress bleeding flesh. Infinite air,
compressed from dizzy altitudes, now serves

his skullface as a pillow. Overhead
a vulture leers in solemn mockery,
knowing what John had never known: that dead
workers are dead before they cease to be.

1928

Winter's Ghost Plagues Them

It is summer, it is warm in the city square:
Lafayette's sword glints in the rich sunlight.
Below him, at the pedestal, men sit smoking,
collars open at neck, discussing winter.

They sprawl, sleeves rolled back, on the hot stone,
they wander, from time to time, to the fountain.
A can of beer is passed from hand to hand
and they swallow deep: the foam frames their faces.

But always their movements sag with the heat:
always they reach for the hip-pocket kerchief,
dabbing wet foreheads, wiping the sweat from
face and throat, thick-veined, heavily breathing.

Beyond them, where grass creeps to dropping tulips
and midget trees rise from soil, dry and leafless,
a lone bird sings; his notes are like scales on
a long-untuned violin, the bow never rosined.

But the men at the statue's base discuss winter,
more real, more threatening than any season,
and winter's hunger and nights spent in doorways
pillowed in paper, seeking of cold stone warmth.

The men move slowly, they scowl at the lightning,
suck long and deep at their pipes. Deep in them
they offer thanks, praying for more warm weather
but winter's ghost plagues them and they fear the fall.

1937

Season of Death

This is the sixth winter:
this is the season of death
when lungs contract and the breath of homeless men
freezes on restaurant window panes—men seeking
the sight of rare food
before the head is lowered into the upturned collar
and the shoulders hunched and the shuffling feet
move away slowly, slowly disappear
into a darkened street.

This is the season when rents go up:
men die, and their dying is casual.
I walk along a street, returning
at midnight from my unit. Meet a man
leaning against an illumined wall
and ask him for a light.
                         His open eyes
stay fixed on mine. And cold rain falling
trickles down his nose, his chin.
"Buddy," I begin . . . and look more closely—
and flee in horror from the corpse's grin.

The eyes pursue you even in sleep and
when you awake they stare at you from the ceiling;
you see the dead face peering from your shoes;
the eggs at Thompson's are the dead man's eyes.
Work dims them for eight hours, but then—
the machines silent—they appear again.

Along the docks, in the terminals, in the subway, on the street,
in restaurants—the eyes
are focused from the river
among the floating garbage
that other men fish for,
their hands around poles
almost in prayer—
wanting to live,
wanting to live! who also soon
will stand propped by death against a stone-cold wall.

1935

WORK AND REVOLUTION

Room with Revolutionists

FOR J.F.

Look at this man in the room before you:
he is young, his skin is dark, his hair
curly and black, his eyes are strangely blue,
he comes from a warmer land under the sun.
He hears a North American speak calmly
of a beautiful and faithless mistress
and is amazed. This man's a revolutionist,
painter of huge areas, editor
of fiery and terrifying words, leader
of the poor who plant, the poor who burrow
under the earth in field and mine.
His life's an always upward-delving battle in
an old torn sweater, the pockets always empty.

And this his companion across the room:
younger than he: the smooth deep forehead
sheathing a subtle and redoubtable brain;
his hair dark, eyes upward-slanting at the corners,
lips clean-etched and full. This man,
nurtured in a northern city,
is a poet, master of strong sensuous words,
artist in his own right. His oratory
before many listeners is like the sudden
startling completeness of summer rain:
warm, clear and clean, soaking into
the very heart of you, the sun just beyond.
This man is my brother, Communist, friend,
counsellor of my youth and manhood. He has crossed
the seething continent a hundred times,
leaving behind him his words
and the sound of them and their meaning.

The heavy drowsy wine of a tropic land
and the sharp bouquet of the northland intermingle
here in this room: these two are held
umbilical to a greater source and destiny,

welded each to each more firmly
than each to his native land.
                              Their vision
parallels their warmth, transcends all frontiers.

Look at them here at ease
relaxed in this pleasant room:
you will not see them again
together for many years.
Tomorrow each will go
his separate way on the maps of the globe
across great distances, talking, painting,
composing poems, organizing,
welding together South- and North-men,
destroying boundaries.

                                              1934

Faces No Longer White

Let something in through the open window.
It is dark here and the floors creak
whenever your bare feet tread on them. Go
to the eye of the crumbling house where your meek
face will be visible to air, to light,
to all that moves intangible in night.
Here is only blackness and stifling air
and a dead face no longer white in its frame
of dim gaslight and black-smudged walls. Go where
seethes the turmoil out of which you came.
Dive into it as you would into a lake
whose depths are thick with tangled stalk and weed:
plunge! Then surge upward, leaving in your wake
a path through which these faces may be freed.

c. 1934

Definition

Knowing this man, who calls himself comrade,
mean, underhanded, lacking all attributes
real men desire, that replenish all worlds
men strive for; knowing that charlatan, fool too,
masquerading always in our colors, must also
be addressed as comrade—knowing these
and others to be false, deficient in knowledge
and love for fellow men that motivates our kind,

nevertheless I answer the salutation proudly,
equally sure that no one can defile it,
feeling deeper than the word the love it bears,
the world it builds. And no man, lying,
talking behind back, betraying trustful friend,
is worth enough to soil this word or mar this world.

1934

WORK AND REVOLUTION

Prophecy in Stone

FOR PAUL STRAND

Enter the ruined hacienda: see Christ
in fifty different tortured poses,
varnished, carved to semblance of life, endowed
with breath almost: here where the camera eye
restores the initial spirit, reveals
the permanence surviving death. Ferret out
a race's history in a finger's curve,
see sun-washed walls flaking to dust,
the dust to powder won by the wind;
deep gashes, rust of rain and sun,
stones fallen, and the black deep grooves
where peons crucified conquistadors,
nailed them to walls, whips clutched
in paralyzed hands tense in agony.

See too the solitary mare
grazing in the barbed enclosure surrounding
the dead mansion of glory: and the mountains
rising beyond, and the pendant clouds
hung in the skies, identical with
horizons Coronado never conquered.

Marks of boot and fingerprint remain
on the rainless scene: nails jut from walls
long cleaned by wind and bird of flesh and bone.
See here, a continent away, the evidence
of grandeur ground to death by time and man,
and the lonely spirit, sun on the anguished eyes
of the carved Christ; and the deep patience
men of another century engraved
on these stone walls and images—lines like words
shouting: "We are enslaved!"
                              lines in prophetic
thunder: "We shall rise,

                    conquer our conquerors."

1936

WORK AND REVOLUTION

The Ship

We shall watch its final plunge from afar,
keeping sinews strong and our minds free
of its sea-soaked rot. We shall be everywhere
when faces turn, fresh-eyed, to the wind:
not here, where decay is constant, but on shores
that beckon as this antique vessel dies.

I do not mean we will desert,
but no ship, sinking, is worth salvaging
in seas where masts are numerous and men are
enough to board them, steer them to port.
We shall be here only to save the living cargo,
carry it untouched to greener shores

while the old vessel, having served its lords,
transporting human vassals and rich plunder,
sinks upon the water, empty, with only
rats running, panic-driven, on its decks;
finally surrenders to the cleansing sea,
weighted with age and its rusty slave chains.

1936

The Burdens of History

To Thine Own Self

If this uncertain living, these days that mount
directionless as terror, haunt us too deeply,
help us to find solutions, to count deeds
well-done which otherwise might fall behind
meaningless as steel tracks speeding in sunlight
unchangingly away in train-momentum's vision.

No words men speak are really, finally, true.
No friend can know nor understand completely.
No woman means everything. No one pursuit
captures the spirit to exclude all others.
And no single star is ever always faithful;
the mariner must lean on compass more than sky.

So freely disavow the proved uncertainties
and seek from self. Perfect an artless guide
to steer unswervingly through seas and woods
and city nightmares. Set the firepoint north
or south: the wind that comes to blow to cool
your captive vision will revive and free it.

May 22nd 1939

When Toller died, the roses at his bier
put forth new thorns of sharpest anger,
warning the mourners with lean and bitter power,
pitying the unhungry valedictorians.
When Toller died, for a moment the world
was quiet, suddenly stilled: the bombs over Barcelona
hung for a shattering second motionless over wild
fearfully beating hearts and eyes fixed skyward.

The speechmakers could not see, beyond the closed lids,
the landscape of horror engraved on the tortured eyes:
the prison yard at Neuburg, the swallow against the bars,
the planes above the olive grove beyond the turning river,
the horizon of Nazi faces murdering Muehsam,
advancing to murder the world—when Toller died.

1939

Recruit

Knowing I leave tomorrow, I look
fondly, finally, around me and drink
all colors and contours deeply, like wine;
press perfect landscape to imperfect memory.

Leaving a well-loved place forever is
like rising a last time from loving or
like closing an unfinished book or seeing
for the last time a friend who is not of this world.

I wanted to leave a part of myself here,
a friend, a wife, a son to grow up among
these trees and valleys and hills I have loved.

But the summons was too sudden
and my time too brief
and my prophets false.

c. 1943

In the Time of Hesitation

What's in the wind? There is no wind.
What's in the air? Dust.
The dust hangs yellow in the stagnant air,
oppressive on the treeless drill-worn fields
where eager boys with ancient eyes
master their manual-of-arms, till soon
instead of group, they call themselves platoon.

Here, under smouldering Texas sun,
summer beginning and training ending,
daily we read the morning headlines,
nightly we turn the dial, listening
for the words that do not come, the deeds
that hang, suspended like dust in air,
over festering *Festung Europa:*
the deeds, millionfold as there are men among us,
but simplest and singular in definition:
some say *invasion,* others *second front.*

And I, one among many, remember
other clouds upon other horizons,
the urgencies of other years and other deeds
which now, so soon, are dust upon the air,
dust wherein the million half-remembered faces
and million haunted eyes accuse without voices,
repeating the agonized question: When? When?

Man's memory is brief, but somewhere, always,
hearts quicken when the word Madrid is spoken
and minds recall its lonely betrayed splendor,
the lost war but the undefeated men
whose hungry flesh became a barricade—
strong, and weak, as steel is strong and weak;
whom treason could not conquer nor hunger weaken
nor bomb nor shell destroy. And now,
imprisoned in the ruins of their immortal city,
their whispers like a huge pulsating wave

beat against the shores of America,
asking: *How soon? How soon?*

Here, on these Texas plains, we simulate
all the innumerable movements of invasion:
down ropes into a hypothetic barge,
from barge to sandy beach, then uphill past
barbed tanglements we cut to let the others by;
then on to the attack. Only combat missing:
actual shell, flesh-mangling bomb, bullet with million eyes.

And I, who have known the muddy embrace of war,
who have lain upon her body of sharpest stone
and trembled with the vast commotion of her passion,
regard these men, my comrades-in-arms, as children
too young to look into her eyes of furious fire,
too innocent to lie in her corrosive arms—
but know how wrong I am when I remember
one hour with her makes men or corpses of us all.
Yes, men or corpses. But Europe cannot wait.
The world cannot wait. And even the Texas plain
will be fertile or scorched, as the war is lost or won.

May 1943

War Guilt

Men dying in battle speak after speech has failed.
Their last mute testaments are written in their eyes:
also their prophecies. These go unrecorded; are
alive only in other men, and die when they die.

I, who survive, remember the eyes of the dying:
their shout as the film closed over: *Traitor, traitor!*
the helpless words: *I accuse.* The rebuke: *You live on.*
Only the rarest times and men the pardon: *I forgive.*

Now with probing foot again we climb the uncertain hill,
each weighted with rifle, pack, biography—
last heaviest of all. Ahead, new explosions
create horizons more vivid than any day.

A man walks calmlier toward night
who carries many midnights in his heart.

At the Moment of Victory

1

At the moment of victory he examines his own heart.
The gun-barrel's cool but the fires still leap
upward from the conquered field, and from his brain
the heat flares in circles and he cannot sleep.
Turbulent and tamed, he remembers those other
countries which are neither victors nor defeated:
those countries of maps and molecules, withered
under neutral sun. Bemedalled and fêted,
he returns to his land-locked starting-point, conscious
he has been well used, like a finely trained stallion.
Now that he's free to graze again, he munches
his cud of applause; but he knows for every million
creatures and men now liberated, other
millions remain under fieldstones, white and smothered.

2

He remembers the fevers, the symptoms of disease.
The electrocardiographic chart records
the preordained murders, the handsome mercenaries
of the corrupt madman and his shrieking words.
And if he is fortunate he will store away
like winter clothes in mothballs the expedient devices:
how to kill with the heel of the hand, and how
to twist the bayonet and throttle dangerous voices.
Devoutly, with all his soul, he hopes—
echoing the diplomats—for a modus vivendi
wherein paths lead peaceward and living shapes
all deeds and words, not only sermons on Sunday.
But the poker chips of profit and of loss,
piled high on the pulpit, hide the preacher's face.

3

He knows, at last, good will is not enough,
complacency a fraud, and that the Golden Rule,
given without measure, can split the deceptive staff
the shepherd leans on, and make of man a tool
in any scoundrel's hand and brain, so finally

he can be shaped to murder or to war:
with all the goodness in the world he soon may be
senseless, corrupted, malevolent as fire—
until the proud boast *Les hommes de bonne volonté*
dies on his chattering lips as he recalls
how all the causes he espoused, existed by,
went singly to their deaths, leaving identical wills
and warnings: without strength and purest purpose they
ask only for betrayal: *Les hommes* sans *volonté.*

1945

Exodus 1947

Midnight, moonlight, most ancient of all seas:
In the heavens, the turbulence of Greco's dreams,
Below, the hull groans, strains, and plows ahead,
The soothing water slaps the steel in innocence.
Imagine the scene: an old ship in an old night
riding the waves of an ancient sea,
carrying an ancient people to an ancient land.

Deep in the vessel's heart, the engines throb
and the hearts of the living cargo throb in sleep,
The night is full of sounds: sounds of breathing,
of dreams of death, of nightmare; all the muted sounds
of a city at midnight. But this city is afloat,
men, women, children, old grandfathers; and all,
all, even the babes in arms, are ancient mariners.

And no light anywhere, for this is an enemy sea.

1947

Idiot Joe Prays in Pershing Square and Gets Hauled in for Vagrancy

Let us praise,
while time to praise remains,
the simple bullet,
the antique ambuscade
and the fanatic justice-crazed assassin—
we who have made
and used napalm
and casually—
alone among all men—
dropped on Man
the only atom bomb.

After Tu Fu (A.D. 713–770)

The innocents were condemned to death in the Hall of Justice.
In the Hall of Peace, the war was declared.
In the name of Mercy, the bomb was dropped on the two cities.
O my maimed brothers, beloved stricken brothers,
dig deep again in the great caves of the East:
again our wise men talk in the Hall of Peace.

The Glory Set

On receiving the full official set of postage stamps
issued by Greece in 1937. Called "The Glory Set,"
since it memorializes ancient Greece, the stamps
draw upon Hellas' proudest legends.

Dear friend, although the stamps are oddly beautiful,
their irony is even more remarkable.
Their origin in a disordered land
kindles my doubt. I cannot understand
the self-destroying wars my long-loved Greece
persists in, not alone since Pericles
but also (a time I still can tune my lyre on)
the age—it's only yesterday!—of Byron.
No matter. Thank you for the gift and, far above it
by peaks of feeling, the affection of it,
knowing affection oftentimes transcends
the fabulous births, the sad and absurd ends
of noblest nations and of dearest friends.

Between these engravings and the Golden Age,
between the artist and his diminutive page,
a Stygian river rages, its tide afoam
with night, and blood, and unrepentant Time:
two long millennia, unrecoverable
in men's imaginings, or art, or will.
These miniatures, that bear the simplest speech
of simple men to points beyond their reach,
confuse us with their beauty, as a gun's
bullet, though small, cuts off all whirling suns
from a soldier's dying vision. Too late
these tributes flower from a desert state
that once was green in man's first blossoming,
when Æschylus and his chorus mimed and sang
the tragic ways of man, his flesh and bone,
and Phidias unlocked the secret of all stone.

Now, though this copied beauty still amazes,
it's coined by politicians, not by muses

who long ago abandoned this rocky, arid
peninsula for pleasanter lands, and married
peoples less obsessed with ancient Greats,
who challenge the living, not the moribund Fates,
to carve from harsher elements the contours
of breathing beasts, not legendary centaurs;
who break the dead-hand grip of fabled glory
and, pulses passionate, create a hardier story
wherein our own tangential visions can
turn all dead gods to living, acting men.

On Rico LeBrun's Crucifixion

Caged in the carnal canvas like a sea
enclosed in gunboats by the metalled man,
it writhes, groans, pivots on its axis
like Christ, His formal cakewalk up to Calvary.

And all the false-faced followers, who cry
"Save our Saviour!" spin on their webbed feet,
mimicking cries of mercy, but their eyes,
blinded with clarity, are hard, are dry.

The flaming arms grope skyward, and the sky
plummets to lowest mankind, asking What?
Be true? Be lizard? Be like Pavlov's rat
beating your brains against the iron door?

Or like ennobled man, defile, betray
your inmost image.
               And befoul
the rare jewels that millennia bear up.

1951

Mystery

The corpse is in the central square, in the spring sun.
The hilts of two jewelled daggers tremble on her breasts.
The blood is cold, corked, on her black and rigid nipples.
Her face in death is beautiful. She has obviously been raped.

Around her walk the busy men, their heads filled with figures.
The women go by with their empty baskets, obsessed with menus,
with many mouths, with the ancient alchemy of mothers
transmuting lead to gold and coppers into bread.

Only the pigeons and the anarchic children hover around her,
the doves bemoaning the death and the child-eyes grave
on the casual brutal bier. All others hurry past.
The sight is familiar as dust in the city air.

Somewhere, it is assumed, an invisible detective
broods darkly in a dark room, his black shoes on the desk,
assuring and reassuring no one in particular
with slow words and fumbling words, in the ritual of despair:

"Sooner or later, mark my word, we'll identify the woman,
and from that to finding the killer is just a small step . . ."
Only the children stand silent, and stare, stare
at the broken body, the lifeless face, the living opulent hair.

c. 1951

Mystery II

Unlike the neat dénouement in the popular novel,
the mystery is never adequately explained:
why the lad with the brilliant I.Q. ended up in a hovel;
why, when the lovers set out on their picnic, it suddenly, brutally rained.

And the sold-out innocent can never understand
how the Fates, that conspired against him, that turned him into a sot,
were simply the normal doing of his best, his truest friend
who, promising all things faithfully, quite naturally forgot.

The final chapter, as usual, long-looked-forward-to,
is strangely, predictably ripped from the overweight book—
so what can we, dear frustrated readers, think or do
who invariably find the richest prize in the hands of the crook,

the lovely virgin with the dazzling hair won by the diseased roué,
and all our golden Tomorrows wrecked on the boneyard of Today?

c. 1951

Kill the Umpire!

He's the infallible man:
calm, caller of balls and strikes,
hits and errors, fair and foul.
He tells us when we're safe or out.

Each of us desires his favor.
Each has his enemy, his chosen side.
We need not only the big battalions
of bats, but also the aid of God.

And he *is* God. We worship him when
his word delights our partisan eyes.
But when his justice moves the other way
we rage, we fume, we shout for his blood.
We would follow him home, if we could, through swarming
streets, through alleys, suburbs, country lanes,
creep up on him from behind and kill him—bang!—
with a pop-bottle. We always kill God.

But since we cannot reach him, we're content
to murder him in our thoughts, to shout
Unfair, unfair! Buy him a pair of glasses!
He's blind as a bat!
                        But the game goes on
according to its rules, which he upholds
by eye, by arm, by his called decision.

Each game has its own peculiar laws
and each its own direction, history;
and he who calls the critical turns
is a lonely man, a man without a country,
a prophet without honor in his own land.

We who sit in the grandstand, watching
the home team lose the heart-breaking close ones,
revile him, damn him—the solitary man—
stare at him, dressed in black like a judge,
his face encased in the steel-wired mask,
the eyes behind it steady, wise;

fearing, knowing the outcome, yet
powerless to prevent the sure defeat.

We sit and watch in outraged silence.
We hate him because whatever he says is true.

Poem

Consciousness, said Don Miguel, *is a disease,*
thus with one huge untruth demolishing
the thousand wisdoms of a jewelled life;
belied his precious broodings, all his
poems of love and loss. Foretold, forefelt
by twenty years the coming of that evil
no-man with his humanless mystique

Consciousness is a disease. The philosophic
cart pulls the nag, destroys the moving beast,
brings death where life was. It is as if
the stranger, lost in the gaunt hills
of a gray uncharted country, heard a wild
amplified shriek upon the air, and then himself
in pain cried out, the echo evoking the cry.

Night World

The lovers tremble in the lost night,
their eyes blurred with torment, their lips
glazed with the moon and kisses. They sleep
unquietly, their senses seared with memory.

Outside their bridal catacomb the moon
rides the cloud-stallions, angry, bucking
the vindictive heavens. The moon remembers too
his own treason to the trusting world;

knows that numberless children, still alive,
will deem him enemy, remembering
his guidance of the plummeting plane, and his
betrayal of their slumbers, mothers, dreams.

The lovers shudder among thorns: their eyes
glisten in the dark, till sleep again
bombards their bodies—and a lone dream-misted eye
rides its own beam to the most distant star.

Dawn Song

The dusk of dawn, the prophet called it:
that birth-hush of gray when from the eastern sky
the colors spill and spread as from a careless
primitive's palette; and overhead
the trees whose invisible branches moaned the whole night long
leap suddenly to green;
and greenest, purest song
bursts forth from the frail throats
of delicate birds. Alas, too soon, too late
the dawn comes on
and wakes the sleeping world
and breaks on me.

But I, its sole insomniac, in a drugged trance,
having reversed the old inheritance
of prehistoric ancestors, cry out
with pallid joy;
and find myself, a modern mariner,
becalmed in the clamorous morning.
Unlike those savages
who dragged themselves to darkest holes to die,
I long to die in daylight. And to this desire
all night in travail I fight the windmill pain
of breathing, living, of my treasonous heart
that pounds the blood like lacerating drums
through the dark deltas of my arteries
and brain. At last it comes,
too late, too soon, the dawn:
and wakes all life and calms me into sleep.

At my small window
the violet glows, and the invading gold
startles my room with coldest sun. Outside,
across the avenue as narrow as a shroud,
the memorized landscape wakes anew.
A lone sparrow sings a raucous madrigal
from his red podium; then, flying, soars
the sudden sky of day, graceful, aflight,

a stone's throw distant, but with no thought of stone,
no consciousness of anything but dawn,
a bird's dawn, wherein no human thought
or pain or joy or waking plays a part,
nor of this heart that, with its world
of friends and loves and acts and memories,
pounds on toward certain doom.

The dawn comes with its birds and forebodings,
wakes all the sleeping world in a fever of trembling.
I rise from bed, force the granite from my chest.
We argue, body and myself, for mastery,
and I know we are all on the brink of a smiling, delicate disaster.
Nevertheless I bathe, I dress, I smile at my wife,
do all the expected things, in the early dawn,
as I hear the beating wings swoop down
on all the world; and take my vitamin pill
and pretend I see no ends, only beginnings,
and that all is undoubtedly right,
all's magically well.

c. 1952

Bon Voyage

Permit me refuge in a region of your brain:
carry and resurrect me, whatever path you take,
as a ship creates its own unending wake
or as rails define direction in a train.

Permit my memory refuge: but not the recent years
when grains of dross obscured the bars of truth.
Delve deeper back in years to your first youth,
passionate, clean, untarnished by small fears.

And if your conscience truly bears my memory,
rekindle if you can the dying candle-light:
let the wake not lose its contour, nor the bright
reflected sun waver as the rails glide by.

My wake and rail attend you, welded and wed,
through the blind tunnels of the years ahead.

c. 1952

Summons to the
Inquisition

Now the Fog

Now the fog falls on the land.
Imagination's eyes go blind.
And the smoke, sole residue of written wisdom,
bears poet and prophet to their doom,
their grave, their wavering edgeless tomb.

Knaves masqued like sovereigns decree
what we shall say, listen to, see.
The habit of slavery, long discarded,
becomes our normal comfortable suit.
Soon we will savor the spoiled fruit
as taste-buds wither on nerveless tongues.
The belly will defeat the brain
in combat perfunctory and painless,
and the gutted brain not find it hard
to crawl inside the colorless Pale
of a stamped official registration card.

And this was the land that Ponce found
seeking his lost youth; the land
young mariners, following old stars, set free . . .

The fog falls, settles, seeps into the land
among the despairing, the despised, the blind;
and only rare and blest oases of courage
mark the blurred landscape, lest even the iron
rust—in all of us, agèd and young—
of the English tongue.

1950

SUMMONS TO THE INQUISITION

The Poisoned Air Befouled the Whole Decade

The poisoned air befouled the whole decade,
corrupting even those whose childhood vision
contained no hint of bomb or nuclear fission,
backed them against walls, cowering, afraid.

Even the purest in heart were daily bombarded
with the subtlest lies and slanders, so that at last
the grip of their fingers slipped from the main mast
of their lives' integrity; and, shoddily rewarded
with glasses to squint through, sticks to lean upon,
soiled coins to buy their bogus luxuries,
they tottered, well-fed hirelings, to the grave.

Knowing this, I choose fondly to remember one
who, victim like the others, nevertheless gave
no quarter to the blackguards and their infamies;
held up his wounded face, looked through his pierced eyes,
saying, Truth is everywhere truth, lies always lies.

September 30, 1949

In Praise Of

To understand the strength of those dark forces
phalanxed against him would have spelled surrender:
the spiked fist, the assassin's knife, the horses'
eyeless hooves above as he fell under.
To understand the sum of all this terror
would *a priori* have meant defeat, disaster.
Born of cold panic, error would pile on error,
heart and mind fall apart like fragile plaster.

Therefore I honor him, this simple man
who never clearly saw the threatening shapes, yet fought
his complex enemies, the whole sadistic clan,
persistently, although unschooled. Untaught,
he taught us, who could talk so glibly, what
the world's true shape should be like, and what not.

All Ghouls' Night

Goaded by outraged Soul,
    Conscience conspired
to kill the two-faced Ghoul
    both of them feared.

Compounded of deceit
    and avarice and horror,
shrieking *I am the state,*
    Ghoul unleashed his terror,

destroyed all loveliness.
    Instead seals agony
on Soul's astonished face
    and anguished body.

Now, as the girl expires,
    Repeat after me, Ghoul
prompts, *and walk through fire*
    to save yourself, damned Soul.

And stricken Soul, complying,
    turned to Truth and said:
Though my actual beauty dies,
    this sacrificial deed

love always, for my death,
    though cruel, is pure,
and my expiring breath
    kindles a cleaner fire

in which some day all Ghouls
    themselves will turn
on sulphurous spits and foul,
    and only Lies will burn.

July 26, 1951

Ballad of the Noble Intentions

What will you do, my brother, my friend,
    when they summon you to their inquisition?
I'll fire from the heart of my fortress, my brain,
    my proudest possession.

And what will you say, my brother, my friend,
    when they threaten your family's food instead?
Like Christ, I'll be silent. Man does not live
    only by work or by bread.

I will think of the poets who fashioned my mind,
    of the singing strokes of my vivid Old Masters,
of the meaning of my own works. These outweigh
    all minor disasters.

And what if your treasures are trampled by swine?
    What if they foul your art and your science?
I'll answer with anger, go down, if I must,
    hurling pearls of defiance.

I will answer with anger, speak up with passion,
    defy them again with my famed indignation.
But what if they babble of danger, and cite
    the imperilled nation?

For it's *they* who imperil our country, my friend,
    they are the worms at the core of the matter.
How will you answer their glib accusations,
    their hypocrite chatter?

I've only contempt for these cloven-tongued men,
    these pack-rats that roam our land in committees
with their claques and their clatter, spreading their lies
    through our sleeping cities.

I will stand like an oak in maturity, like
    a craft of fine timber against the sea's fury.
But what if these little men posture and act
    as both judge and jury?

I'll read them bold pages from Areopagitica,
quote Milton and Marvell to rout and abuse them.
The best words of men of all ages will rise
to my tongue to confuse them!

*   *   *

And what did you do, dear brother, dear friend,
when you stood at last in the pygmies' forum?
I spoke with good sense, old friend, I talked with
restraint and decorum.

I decided that boasting like Milton were vain,
or refusing, like Marvell, their guineas with anger.
I patterned myself after Waller, who lived
more richly—certainly longer.

I engaged them in skilful debate, since I felt
that mere youthful defiance was unrealistic.
I told what I knew, or I thought, to be true;
it was harmless, anachronistic.

And what did you say, dear brother, old friend?
What were the truths you hastened to utter?
Not words—just a disinterred corpse from a grave,
on a neutral platter.

And there were some living men too that I named.
What harm could it do them, after two decades?
Besides, as I've reason to know, it was all—
after all—in the records.

Just look at the transcript, dear brother, dear friend.
Is there anything in it to make a man shudder?
Is there anything there to make anyone think
that I've lost my rudder?

No, nothing at all, dear stranger, lost friend,
    nothing to move me to grief or to mourning.
It's yourself you betrayed, it's yourself who lives on
    as a living warning.

Your act of survival betrayed *not* your friends,
    but yourself most of all—no need now to cavil.
Live on, as you must, but be happy with Waller,
    not Milton, or Marvell.

For you've toppled the bridges you had with your youth,
    your promising present and excellent future.
No masterpiece ever can heal such a wound, nor
    a surgeon's suture.

You killed your own scope, sad stranger, lost friend.
    My affection is dead; it's too frayed now, and grieving.
And *that* was your crime; in the noon of your life
    you resigned from the living.

                            1952

Political Prisoner 123456789

I heard this man called traitor, I saw him shamed
before his friends, forsaken by companions;
his wealth and worth destroyed, his picture in the papers,
the caption cautioning "Beware, this man's an enemy."
His age, description given, his children named, his wife
mentioned profanely, his private habits exposed;
the walls of his few rooms torn wide for all to see,
the walls of his life's efforts crumbling, broken—

—yet knew the deed was a lie, the accusations false,
the men whose mouths uttered them not fit to tread
the same earth he walked, nor able to oppose him
by other means than falsehood. They lied to save themselves.
This man is still my friend. And thousands more,
in their truest thoughts and acts, daily do him honor.

A Poem to Delight My Friends Who Laugh at Science-Fiction

That was the year
the small birds in their frail and delicate battalions
committed suicide against the Empire State,
having, in some never-explained manner,
lost their aerial radar, or ignored it.

That was the year
men and women everywhere stopped dying natural deaths.
The agèd, facing sleep, took poison;
the infant, facing life, died with the mother in childbirth;
and the whole wild remainder of the population,
despairing but deliberate, crashed in auto accidents
on roads as clear and uncluttered as ponds.

That was the year every ship on every ocean,
every lake, harbor, river, vanished without trace;
and even ships docked at quays
turned over like harpooned whales, or wounded Normandies.

Yes, and the civilian transcontinental planes
found, like the war-planes, the sky-lanes crowded
and, praising Icarus, plunged to earth in flames.

Many, mild stay-at-homes, slipped in bath tubs,
others, congenital indoors-men, descending stairs,
and some, irrepressible roisterers, playing musical chairs.
Tots fell from scooter cars and tricycles
and casual passersby were stabbed by falling icicles.

Ah, what carnage! It was reported
that even bicarb and aspirin turned fatal,
and seconal too, to those with mild headaches,
whose stomachs were slightly acid, or who found they could not sleep.
All lovers died in bed, as all seafarers on the deep.

Till finally the only people left alive
were the soldiers sullenly spread on battlefields
among the shell-pocked hills and the charred trees.
Thus, even the indispensable wars died of ennui.

But not the expendable conscripts: they remained as always.
However, since no transport was available anywhere,
and home, in any case, was dead, and bare,
the soldiers wandered eternally
in their dazed, early-Chirico landscapes,
like drunken stars in their shrinking orbits
round and round and round and round

and (since I too died in the world-wide suicide)
they may still, for all I know, be there.
Like forsaken chessmen abandoned by paralyzed players.
they may still be there,
may still be there.

A Hunter Went Killing:
A Fable

The small birds flew from tree to tree
    at the shore of the blue lake far below.
Cold was the day; and singing, free,
the swallows darted from tree to tree.

Small, insignificant creatures, they
    played in the green leaves carelessly,
swift as all life is. Cold was the day,
perfect for song and flight and play.

A hunter strode to the lake's shore,
    sighted his gun toward the sky, and fired.
Some birds fled crying, and many more
lay bleeding on the blue lake's shore.

The hunter stood at the edge of the water
    and fired and reloaded ceaselessly.
Tears fell from his eyes beside the water—
from the smoke? the cold? the small birds' slaughter?

Said one bird to another: "Look! He cries
    as he fires his firearm endlessly.
The tears run streaming from his eyes
each time a wingèd brother dies."

The other replied to his merciful friend:
    "Never mind his eyes, nor his flowing tears.
Think of sky, not the earth where the hunter stands.
Don't pity his weeping. Watch his hands."

January 13, 1953

SUMMONS TO THE INQUISITION

Words Found on a Cave's Wall

The time came, at last, when only two things had meaning:
friendship, for compassion; consolation, for love;
the time when only harshest animal warmth
kept us, and our hope, alive in the dark caves
of the soul's winter.

For they, who had the strength
to kill all thought, all spirit, with their savage scalpels,
went mad with their own power's impotence
against our fragile flowering granite. And how better
kill an idea than crush the inseparable flesh
which is its womb, its cradle, and its soil?

Nevertheless we endured in the long darkness,
sharing our warmth and our desperate hopes
in the mole-tunnels of our catacombs;
yet never, quite, amid despair,
never quite lost the fertilizing hope
nor surrendered the clear and kindling idea
that shone serene as candle-light in the gathering gloom,
that some day all false idols would be shattered,
all repressions lifted, all
the cudgel-wielders fall under the double weight
of our steadfastness and their savagery.

The year, dear never-to-be-known stranger,
is not, alas, the year that you read this.
It is three centuries and a decade
since the death of Him Whom they will not acknowledge.
The place is Rome. The Emperor's Constantine.
The catacombs we live in, and die in, are real.
And these farewell words, unborn reader, friend perhaps,
are both our epitaph and prophecy.

September 20, 1951

Are You Now or Have You Ever Been

I admit it: there was a moment of pity
a vulnerable second of sympathy
my defenses were down
and I signed the letter asking clemency
for the six Negroes the letter
hereinafter known as Exhibit A

I signed the letter yes
the signature is indubitably mine
and later this at another time
I wrote a small check yes small
since my income is small
perhaps ten dollars not more
for the fund these people were collecting
to keep the refugees alive

and then again in a moment of weakness
I promised and kept my promise
to join the demonstration at the city hall
protesting the raising of rents
no you needn't show me the photograph
I was there I admit I was there

but please   believe me
everything I did was done through weakness if you will
but it's strange how weakness of this kind snowballs
multiplies
before they approached me with that innocent petition
I was may it please the court exactly
like you like every other man
I lived my own life solely suffered
only my own sorrows and enjoyed my own triumphs
small ones I grant you
asked nothing from
gave nothing to
any man
except myself my wife my children

so there you have it
it is all true
Exhibits A and B and C
and the witnesses don't lie
I wanted to help those six men stay alive
I thought them innocent
I honestly believed the rents were too high
(no, I own no tenements)
and the anguish of the refugees starving far from home
moved me I admit more than it should have
perhaps because I still retain
a fleeting childhood picture of my great grandfather's face
he too was a refugee

c. 1953

A Letter to the Denouncers

Dear sir: the summum bonum is
Solvency, which sufficiently defined most simply means
Spuds in sufficient quantities,
an untapped phone, and daily pork and beans.

Sir, as you start for work each morning, please
check your clothes-closet for skeletons,
your dreams for inconsistencies,
the radio in your car for microphones.

This too remember: old man, tired man, fool,
after their final sessions with their analysts,
shape all their Methods to one glowing Goal—
Safety. And so they draw up lists.

And *what* lists! One, born of maliciousness,
another of envy, a third of gratitude—
name first the friend who straightened out their mess,
then him who found them work, and self-respect, and bread.

Naturally they're honest; they've merely changed their views.
They flinch before the paradox of Means and Ends.
So, hating dubious Means, each casually betrays
his benefactors, boon-companions, friends.

A crazy crowd applauds these eager choristers
who sing as wingless birds have never sung before.
But you, dear friendless friends, dear lonely sirs,
recall whom *you*'ve befriended, and beware, beware.

c. 1953

1949 (After Reading a News Item)

His first official act was to bless
The planes that bombed their Barcelona home.
Ten years have passed. Today his Holiness
Welcomes the Catalan orphans into Rome.

June 19, 1953

This court, supreme in blindness and in hate,
supremely flaunts its lickspittle estate;
kills Jews today, as twenty-five years ago,
it killed Italians.

Pastoral—1954

Who used to lie with his love
        In the glade, far from the battle-sector,
        Now lies embraced by a lie-detector
And can not, dare not, move.

Ballad

What are we having for dinner tonight?
Whom are we having for dinner tonight?
        Raw nerve ends on toast
        Pickled cops' feet
        Suckling pig with a gag in its mouth
        And no talk—its ears are wired for sound.

Little Ballad for Americans—1954

Brother, brother, best avoid your workmate—
Words planted in affection can spout a field of hate.

Housewife, housewife, never trust your neighbor—
A chance remark may boomerang to five years at hard labor.

Student, student, keep mouth shut and brain spry—
Your best friend Dick Merriwell's employed by the F.B.I.

Lady, lady, make your phone calls frugal—
The chief of all Inquisitors has ruled the wire-tap legal.

Daughter, daughter, learn soon your heart to harden—
They've planted stoolies everywhere; why not in kindergarten?

Lovers, lovers, be careful when you're wed—
The wire-tap grows in living-room, in auto, and in bed.

Give full allegiance only to circuses and bread;
No person's really trustworthy until he's dead.

                                                    1954

Cary Nelson

The Spanish Civil War

"First Love"

This poem was written in 1943 while Rolfe was in training in Texas after being drafted by the U.S. Army. See the Introduction. When first published in *Yank: The Army Weekly* in 1945, Rolfe titled it "First Love (Remembering Spain)." The parenthetical addition to the title may have been intended not only to alert readers to its Spanish referent but also to allude to Louis MacNeice's poem "Remembering Spain," which has a number of points of similarity with "First Love." MacNeice, for example, remembers "fretwork that the Moor / Had chiselled for effects of sun and shadow." MacNeice's poem's final lines have since become a touchstone for the commitment to Republican Spain:

> And next day [I] took the boat
>> For home, forgetting Spain, not realizing
> That Spain would soon denote
>> Our grief, our aspirations;
> Not knowing that our blunt
>> Ideals would find their whetstone, that our spirit
> Would find its frontier on the Spanish front,
>> Its body in a rag-time army.

See the Introduction and its notes for further information.

"A Federico García Lorca"

Rafael Alberti and María Teresa Leon were both Spanish writers and were married to each other. Langston Hughes was in Madrid regularly in the fall of 1937. Rolfe spent a good deal of time with Alberti and Hughes while he was in Madrid editing *Volunteer for Liberty,* scheduling radio broadcasts, and serving as American political commissar. See Cary Nelson and Jefferson Hendricks, *Edwin Rolfe: A Biographical Essay and Guide to the Rolfe Archive at the University of Illinois at Urbana-Champaign* (1990), for further information about Rolfe's relationship with Hughes, including a 1937 poem that Hughes wrote and dedicated to Rolfe. Rolfe first met Alberti and Teresa Leon in New York in 1935, at which time he wrote a story on them for the *Daily Worker.* The last line of Rolfe's poem alludes to García Lorca's "Ballad of the Spanish Civil Guard": "They ride the roads with souls of patent leather." Rolfe kept a clipping of Hughes's translation of the poem.

"Epitaph"

This poem was originally published as "For Arnold Reid." Reid was a classmate of Rolfe's at the University of Wisconsin. Rolfe describes his death in *The Lincoln Battalion:* "On a hill adjacent to the Lincoln position another American—one of the most competent and mature and kindly of all in Spain—died as he directed the fire of a machine-gun in his company. He was Arnold Reid, a twenty-six-year-old American who had worked for many years in South and Latin America, and who had joined the Spanish Battalion of the Fifteenth Brigade in order to strengthen the work of the many Latin Americans in its ranks. The Spaniards, especially the young *quintos,* had loved the quiet young man who had become commissar of their machine-gun company; who knew their language and songs and traditions as well, if not better, than any of them, who treated them like a kind and just father. The Lincolns heard of his death for the first time when Joseph North, first of the correspondents to reach the Ebro lines, visited the battalion during a momentary lull in the fighting on July 29th. The news stunned them more than the news of any death ordinarily did" (267). See the Introduction for further comments.

"Death by Water"

Malgrat is a fishing village on the Catalan coast about twenty-two miles north of Barcelona. The ship *Ciudad de Barcelona* had brought international volunteers to Spain on earlier occasions as well, often traveling a route from Marseilles to Alicante. As noted in *International Solidarity with the Spanish Republic* (1975), the ship brought 650 volunteers from many countries to Alicante on October 9, 1936; it brought another group of volunteers from Marseilles to Alicante on October 13. Abe Osheroff describes his experience as a passenger on the *City of Barcelona* when it was torpedoed by a submarine in a passage in *Our Fight: Writings by Veterans of the Abraham Lincoln Brigade* (1987): "I remember a loud, dull thud, and the whole ship sort of shuddered. In a matter of minutes, it tilted sharply and began to go down by the stern. Pandemonium followed as men raced to the very few lifeboats. I remember a loaded lifeboat crashing down on its occupants. I remember the screaming faces of seamen trapped at the portholes. And above all I remember some seamen tearing loose anything that could float and tossing it into the sea. I dived into the water and began to swim away, to avoid being pulled down by the suction. Almost immediately, I felt guilt and swam back to help with the rescue of nonswimming comrades" (85). In *The Lincoln Battalion* Rolfe quotes Sidney Shosteck: "The men died helping each other" (84). Rolfe first called the poem "City of Barcelona" and later retitled it "Death by Water." The final title is an explicit reference to the fourth section of Eliot's *The Waste Land.* In giving the poem that title Rolfe may also have had in mind his friend Sol Funaroff's poem "What the Thunder Said: A Fire Sermon," which was first published in a condensed version in *New Masses* in 1932. The full poem appeared in Funaroff's *The Spider and the Clock* (1938), which Funaroff sent to Rolfe in Spain in June 1938.

"City of Anguish"

This poem is dedicated to Milton Wolff, last commander of the Lincoln Battalion. The feeling behind the dedication may be represented most clearly by the inscription Rolfe wrote in the copy of *The Lincoln Battalion* he gave to Wolff in November 1939: "With deepest admiration and friendship.—Certain qualities remain with a man all his life: things he did, said, thought, felt. What you were and what you did in Spain, Milt, can never be lost; it remains deep in the memory and in the consciousness of all of us who at one time or other were under your command, all of us whose acts were more perfect because you were there with us, leading us. The stature you achieved there—the respect, admiration, love that we had for you, and the confidence and trust you inspired in us, will always be part of us and a part of you in our eyes." Wolff's copy of *The Lincoln Battalion* is included in his archive, which is also at the University of Illinois.

By the time Rolfe arrived in Madrid in the summer of 1937 the city, while still under siege and under bombardment, was no longer the main focus of Franco's military campaign. The poem draws on Rolfe's experience of the city in the summer and fall of 1937 to evoke the Madrid of that year and the previous year as well. In the fall of 1936 Franco sent his own troops and the German Condor Legion to take the city on the ground and break its will by artillery and air bombardment. At some points in November up to two thousand rounds of artillery were fired on Madrid each hour. As the historian Hugh Thomas wrote in *The Spanish Civil War* (1977), the German officers directing the bombardment for Franco "were interested to see the reaction of a civilian population to a carefully planned attempt to set fire to the city, quarter by quarter. The bombing included also buildings such as the Telefónica or the war ministry, whose destruction would cause special damage" (486). Blocks of apartments were destroyed, trees were uprooted, huge bomb craters were left in the roads, fires burned regularly, and thousands of civilians were killed. But the people's will was not broken. And the city was not taken. Following the unsuccessful direct frontal assault, Franco also tried to encircle the city, first from the west and then from the east. The major battles in and around Madrid lasted from November 1936 to March 1937.

 Paseo: literally, a leisurely stroll or promenade. On Sunday many people dressed up for a traditional promenade along major streets or through public squares.

Gran Via: This is the major east-west avenue in Madrid. It was constructed in three sections, the first of which opened in 1924. During the first months of the war, the fascist general Emilio Mola announced that he would be having coffee on the Gran Via by October 12. The general did not keep his rendezvous; thereafter a large printed reservation for him was satirically maintained on a table at the Cafe Molinero on the Gran Via. It was down the Gran Via that the International Brigades marched in November 1936 on their way to the front on the outskirts of Madrid.

 Telefónica: The large modernist-style telephone building, which served as the headquarters of Spain's telecommunications company, was Madrid's highest building when it was erected in 1929. It stands on the Gran Via on the highest ground in the center of the city. Its large red clock still dominates the night skyline. During the war it was an observation post for Republican artillery and for that reason among others also one of the more famous targets in Madrid. It was shelled repeatedly by the rebels and also used as a reference point to aim shells up the Gran Via.

Casa de Campo: This is a sprawling wooded park northwest of the city that was the scene of major fighting during the attacks on Madrid. Its hills and scrub brush made rapid troop movement difficult but provided excellent cover for the Nationalist troops. In the summer of 1936, when terror reigned in both Nationalist and Republican cities, the *Casa de Campo* was the scene of frequent summary executions.

Puerta del Sol (Gateway of the Sun): The arc-shaped *plaza de la Puerta del Sol* is often considered the heart of Madrid and of Spain as well. A number of the major roads in the city have their origin there, and it is also identified as "kilometer zero" for the nation's major highways. Rolfe often walked through the plaza when he was in Madrid in 1937. Both historically and during the Spanish Civil War it was the scene of major political gatherings.

Florída: This was one of two hotels in Madrid—the other being the *Gran Via* (across from the *Telefónica* building)—where journalists frequently gathered during the war. Hemingway stayed there when he was in Madrid in 1937, taking one of the large (and then inexpensive) rooms in the front that faced the fascist artillery. The *Florída* was located on the Plaza Cayou a block west of the *Telefónica* building; after the war the *Florída* was torn down to make way for a department store.

Ryan: An IRA member since 1918, Frank Ryan became the chivalrous leader of the Irish volunteers in the International Brigades. He had the rank of captain and commanded the Irish company of the British Battalion. Captured by fascist forces in the spring of 1938, he was turned over to German troops and later murdered by the Gestapo.

Pasionaria: La Pasionaria (Dolores Ibarruri Gomez) was one of the most famous figures of the Spanish Civil War. Her 1936 radio speech rallying the defenders of Madrid gave the Republic its battle cry: "No Pasaran!" (They Shall Not Pass). She was also deeply involved in all the Spanish Communist party's political maneuvers during the war, but it is her role in the defense of Madrid that Rolfe honors here. She was born in 1895 in a small mining village and politicized by the oppressive sexism of traditional Spanish culture and by the intense poverty of her family. Four of her six children died for lack of food and medicine. Something of her impact on people is captured in this excerpt from Vincent Sheean's comments on her in his text accompanying her portrait in Jo Davidson, *Spanish Portraits* (1938): "It was on the night of July the eighteenth, 1936, when military revolt had blazed out all over Spain, that Dolores spoke over the Madrid radio and proclaimed in her plangent, sad and magical voice, words which are Madrid's forever:

'No pasaran.' Through the long siege she was a force among the people, a force for encouragement, for organization and for hard work. The workers' militias and their successor, the popular army, the women and children of workers, and the government itself owe as much to her as to any individual element at their command. Her words found their way into every Spanish heart and imagination. 'It is better to die on your feet than to live on your knees,' she said, and millions have repeated it through these two years and a half of bitter, exhausting war. . . . She reaches those secret depths because she is herself a collective phenomenon, inseparable from the people for whom and to whom she speaks."

"Casualty"

Tibidábo: This is a 532-meter-high mountain in the foothills on the outskirts of Barcelona. It forms the northwest boundary of the city. Republican anti-aircraft guns were placed there during the war. It is known for the fine views of Barcelona it provides on clear days. The mountain's name is taken from the Latin version of Satan's offer during Christ's Temptations. Satan took him to a high place and offered everything that could be seen below: "Haec omnia tibi dabo si cadens adoraberis me" (All these things I will give thee, if thou wilt fall down and worship me).

"Eyes of a Blind Man"

This is dedicated to Commandante Gabriel Fort, who commanded the Sixth of February Battalion. Seriously wounded in the Jarama campaign, he returned to service and was blinded at Brunete in July 1937. Rolfe wrote the poem after having lunch with Fort in Madrid on Friday, September 3, 1937. Rolfe notes in his diary that a bullet entered one of Fort's eyes and emerged from the other. The epigraph was later revised to commemorate a later meeting with Fort.

"Elegy for Our Dead"

See the Introduction.

"Postscript to a War"

This is dedicated to Michael Gordon, who was stage manager and director for the Theatre Union in New York in the 1930s at the same time as Mary Rolfe was Margaret Larkin's assistant there. Larkin later became a writer and married Albert Maltz. One of the plays Gordon worked on was Maltz's *Black Pit*. Gordon then moved to the Group Theatre. He later worked on Broadway and directed over twenty films in Hollywood. Gordon appeared before the House Un-American Activities Committee as a resistant, uncooperative witness in 1951. In 1958, however, several years after Rolfe's death, he testified in secret and went through the ritual of naming names. See Victor Navasky, *Naming Names* (1980), 276–78, for details.

"Paris—Christmas 1938"

An earlier draft has the title "Lullaby."

"Elegia"

See the Introduction.

Guadarrama winds: Madrid is situated on a 2,120-foot-high plateau, and it is encircled by the Guadarrama Mountains to the north. The winds that sweep down off the mountains are a distinctive part of the city's climate.

"Yes, I weep with Garcilaso": Like Rolfe himself and like some of the young men in the trenches in Madrid, Garcilaso de la Vega (1501–36) was a soldier-poet. In an unpublished essay on poetics, Rolfe mentions that Garcilaso de la Vega's "First Elegy" is one of his favorite poems. His poetic output was small but highly polished, so that he became the undisputed classic poet of the Golden Age of Spanish literature. The recurrent theme in his poetry is love, and the melancholy and frustrated idealism with which it is treated no doubt owes something to his own unrequited love for Isabel Freire, a Portuguese lady-in-waiting to the empress. Rolfe's own love for Madrid here is, of course, frustrated by Franco's domination of Spain. Although the balance of the stanza is addressed to Madrid, the reference to Garcilaso continues to permeate it. The sons and daughters of the city, when they fall in love, are also figuratively children of Garcilaso's romantic poems. Finally, it is worth noting that Garcilaso was mortally wounded when leading an assault on an unimportant but well-fortified position, a story with no lack of parallels to the battles of the Spanish Civil War.

Calle de Velasquez: This is the street where the International Brigades building was located and where Rolfe edited the English-language magazine of the brigades, *Volunteer for Liberty,* from 1937 to the beginning of 1938.

"the green Retiro and its green gardens": Spread out in the middle of Madrid, the Retiro is one of Spain's most beautiful parks. It encompasses a lake and a number of distinct squares, open spaces, and formal gardens. Laid out in the seventeenth century, the park's 320 acres originally served as a royal retreat (*retiro*).

Alcalá: This is a major highway that heads east from its origin in the *Puerta del Sol.* Rolfe often walked along the Alcalá in the fall of 1937. In walking from the International Brigades Headquarters (63 Calle de Velasquez) to the old city, Rolfe would often have walked down Velasquez to Alcalá. The streets meet at the boundary of the Retiro, where Rolfe would have turned west and headed past the massive Puerta de la Alcalá and the Plaza de la Cibeles, past the post office building and the Ministry of Defense, and then on to *Puerta del Sol* and the old part of Madrid. In the 1930s the portion of the Alcalá in the downtown area was the major cafe street in the city.

Gateway to the Sun: This is the *Puerta del Sol,* the central plaza of Madrid. See the notes to "City of Anguish."

Plaza Mayor: A beautifully proportioned, rectangular, seventeenth-century, cobbled, arcaded square. Some 130 yards long and 100 yards wide, it was planned by Felipe II and his architect to serve as a public meeting place for the new capital; it was finished in 1619 during the reign of Felipe III. A 1613 bronze statue of Felipe III on horseback is in the center of the square. The Plaza Mayor has been a frequent site for public spectacles—from processions of flagellants and penitents to bullfights—as well as the site of some of Spain's major public ceremonies—such as the crowning of kings—and the site, finally, of some of its more traumatic historical moments. Thus it was here that the Inquisition held its *autos-da-fé* and executed its victims. Balconies on all four sides of the square provided vantage points for spectators. The Plaza Mayor is located off Calle Mayor a few blocks from *Puerta del Sol.* The streets of Old Madrid radiate from the Plaza Mayor.

Casa de Campo: See the notes to "City of Anguish."

University City: This is the hillside campus of the University of Madrid, which was the scene of dramatic fighting during the struggle for the city. Hoping to end the war quickly with one decisive stroke, Franco ordered a major assault against the Spanish capital in the fall of 1936. After being halted by the people's militias, Franco's troops were preparing additional attacks on the city when the International Brigades marched through Madrid on November 8 to take up positions in their first major battles. On November 9 International Brigade troops spearheaded a counterattack among the gum and ilex trees of the Casa de Campo. In a series of bloody bayonet charges ending in hand-to-hand combat, the Internationals helped retake portions of the park, though Nationalist troops remained entrenched there. A week later the Internationals were engaged in hand-to-hand combat in University City, much of which was reduced to rubble in the process. Buildings were sandbagged; doors and windows were barricaded. Machine guns swept all the open approaches. At one point the ground floor of one building was held by the Thaelmann Battalion of the Internationals and the other floors by Franco's Moors. On another day one room in the Hall of Philosophy changed hands four times. The battle for University City continued until November 23; the fascist advance had been stopped, but University City remained divided between the opposing armies for the rest of the war. The grounds were deeply entrenched, tunnels were dug under streets exposed to fire, and various buildings remained in either Nationalist or Republican hands.

Gypsy Ballads: This refers to *Romancero Gitano* (1928), a book of poems by Federico García Lorca that Rolfe acquired in Albacete in 1937. García Lorca was murdered by Nationalist partisans just after the outbreak of the Spanish Civil War.

Poetas en la España Leal and *Romanceros de los Soldados en las Trincheras:* These are two of a number of poetry anthologies issued in Spain by Loyalist supporters during the war. *Poetas en la España Leal,* containing forty-four poems, was published in July 1937 to honor the Second International Congress of Antifascist Writers, which met in Spain that year. It was compiled by the editors of the journal *Hora de España,* which had previously published most of the poems in the book. Rolfe's entry in his diary for September 11, 1937, notes that he purchased three copies of *Poetas en la España Leal* in Madrid that day.

Portraits

"Eyes of a Boy"

See the opening quotation of the Introduction for another reference to Hilario. Rolfe also writes about Hilario in *The Lincoln Battalion:* "Many of the young, new recruits who joined the decimated American battalion were from Valencia and Alicante. . . . Others were Catalans, schoolboys and young farm and city workers. . . . There was one particularly—Hilario was his first name, nineteen years old and a Catalan—who delighted in singing outlandish renditions of American jazz. For a while he was battalion bugler. . . . Hilario's eyes would gleam with pride and professional solidarity. . . . Hilario lived to be almost twenty years old" (231–33). Rolfe's holograph manuscript for "Eyes of a Boy," dated August 25, 1937, does not include the dedication to Hilario. The dedication lists Hilario's age as fifteen, whereas *The Lincoln Battalion* lists it as nineteen. There are a number of possible explanations—there may have been more than one boy with the same name, Rolfe may have altered names to protect family members from fascist reprisals—but no information has been uncovered to settle the issue.

Valentín González: He was also known as "El Campesino" (the peasant). Originally a guerrilla leader, he became a commander of one of the Mixed Brigades and one of the most famous officers of the Spanish Civil War. Lawrence A. Fernsworth concludes his description of Gonzalez in Davidson's *Spanish Portraits* (1928) as follows: "He gathered together a little company of nineteen men and led them out into the Sierra Guadarrama to hold the road to Madrid on that first day. Later he formed a battalion which made history in the Sierra, defending its position to the last inch and the last man. It was El Campesino's battalion, too, that held the trenches of Carabanchel in the defense of Madrid. His battalion has been in the bloodiest battles since—the defense of Madrid, Villavieja, Buitrago, Quijorna, Brunete, Teruel. At thirty-three he is now commander of a division—a great, black-bearded, rough, laughing, blustering soldier whose name is a word to swear by in the army of the Republic." Also see Rolfe's essay about El Campesino, "Spain's Shirt-Sleeve General," published in the December 7, 1937, issue of *New Masses,* which gives a detailed account of a day Rolfe spent with El Campesino's division in a town near Madrid. Merino and Policarpo commanded the Second and First Brigades under Campesino, who headed the 46th Division. Policarpo Candon was a Cuban-American; his brigade was a mobile shock brigade.

"The Melancholy Comus"
For information on Rolfe's relationship with Chaplin see Nelson and Hendricks, *Edwin Rolfe*.

"Essay on Dreiser (1871–1945)"
This poem was written in Beverly Hills, California, on December 29, 1945, the day after Dreiser died.

"Vincent"
Earlier drafts are titled "Van Gogh." The Borinage is the poor mining district in Belgium where Van Gogh served as a lay minister from 1878 until he was relieved of his duties the following year. The poem includes references to a number of Van Gogh's better-known paintings, from *The Potato Eaters* in the first stanza to *Crows over a Wheatfield* and *Van Gogh's Bedroom* in the third.

"Nuthin but Brass"
Cab Calloway, extravagant singer, dancer, and band leader, was, of course, one of the notable figures of jazz's big band era and perhaps the most popular black entertainer of the 1930s. "Minnie the Moocher" was his signature song, and Rolfe builds allusions to it into his poem. Thus the third verse begins "She had a dream about the King of Sweden. / He gave her things that she was need'n," while the fourth verse ends "She had a million dollars worth of nickels and dimes. / She sat around and counted them all a million times."

Work and Revolution

"Catalogue of *I*"
Rolfe is partly writing a revolutionary version of Whitman's "Song of Myself." He may also have had in mind Langston Hughes's "Let America Be America Again."
"the cotton-clad exile in the caves of loess": Loess is a wind-blown mineral deposit associated with glaciers in the Northern Hemisphere. In China, there are loess deposits that reach five hundred feet in height that include innumerable cave dwellings. Rolfe's reference is to the Chinese revolution. Under attack by Chiang Kai-shek, Mao Tse-tung was forced to abandon his people's republic in southeast China in 1934. After the arduous and epic six-thousand-mile "Long March" of 1934–35, Mao and his followers took

up residence in caves of loess in Shensi province in northwest China. They were clad in native common cloth of rough cotton. Between 1937 and 1945 Mao's communists employed mobile, rural-based guerrilla warfare against the Japanese.

"Asbestos"

The poem was titled "The 100 Percenter" when first published in the *Daily Worker* in 1928. It was retitled "Asbestos" for its 1933 reprinting in *We Gather Strength*.

"Season of Death"

This poem was first published in a longer version titled "The Sixth Winter." See Rolfe's *Collected Poems* for "The Sixth Winter."

"Room with Revolutionists"

This poem is based on a conversation between *New Masses* editor, poet, and Left journalist Joseph Freeman (1897–1965) and the Mexican painter David Alfaro Siqueros (1896–1974). Siqueros was a revolutionary socialist who was politically active both in Mexico and abroad. Freeman went on to write novels and an autobiography. Since Rolfe's admiration for Freeman and Siqueros is based partly on their ability to function, respectively, as writer or artist and revolutionary, it may be useful to give some examples of this double life as each man lived it.

As a young man, beginning in 1914, Siqueros fought in the Mexican revolution. A period of art studies in Europe followed. He returned to Mexico in 1922 to complete such paintings as *Burial of a Worker*, but three years later abandoned painting to devote himself to union organizing and leading mine workers' strikes. In prison in 1930 he began painting again, producing works like *Visit to an Imprisoned Peasant* and later *Proletarian Mother*. In 1932 he accepted exile in the United States, where he remained for two years. He returned to Mexico in 1934 to become president of the National League against Fascism and War. In 1936 he organized a painting workshop in New York and later that year journeyed to Spain to fight in support of the Spanish republic.

Freeman was born in the Ukraine and came to the United States as a young child. A Zionist in his youth, Freeman was a committed socialist by the time he was fifteen. At Columbia University he became active in the antiwar movement during World War I. After graduation he spent two years in Europe as a correspondent, returning to New York to work for *The Liberator* in 1922. Three years later he published *Dollar Diplomacy* with Scott Nearing and the following year founded *New Masses*. He then went to the Soviet Union, where he served for a time as a translator for the Comintern. After returning to the United States in 1927, he coauthored *Voices of October* (1930), which presented the revolutionary art and literature he had encountered in the USSR. Freeman continued to be a prominent intellectual on the Left and in the Party in the first half of the 1930s, but the positive view of

Trotsky in his 1936 autobiography *An American Testament* put him in disfavor in the Soviet Union. At first he was simply compelled to help suppress attention for the book, but when he refused an assignment to write an article on the Moscow trials the following year, relations with the Party began to deteriorate more rapidly. In 1939 *An American Testament* was attacked in the *Communist International* and Freeman was expelled. See the Introduction for further comments.

"Definition"
See the Introduction.

"Prophecy in Stone"
The poem is not only dedicated to Paul Strand but also, as Rolfe notes in the version published in *The Nation,* based on one of Strand's photographs. The image Rolfe had in mind was most likely Strand's 1932 photograph *Beyond Saltillo,* but Rolfe clearly drew inspiration from the rest of Strand's Mexican sequence as well, including the photographs of images of Christ. Rolfe and Strand knew one another well in the 1930s. Leo Hurwitz wrote an introduction to a folio-sized album of Strand's photographs that was included in Rolfe's library.

"see Christ / in fifty different tortured poses": The following note from Rolfe's archive, written several years later, helps clarify this image: "We lifted the injured man to the stretcher; his face was the face of a wounded Christ. Not the diluted Christ of the popular chromos, but the authentic man, the Jeshua of Nazareth, the man whom all peoples everywhere see as themselves, as one of their own. Once, I remember, I saw a carved image of a Christ in Mexico, and it was the face of a Mexican peon, the hair black and matted with sweat and suffering under the thorns, the eyes dark and smouldering with pain, the mouth and the lines about it reflecting the simple, protracted agony of a lifetime of crucifixion in slavery, not the dramatic momentary agony of a quick crucifixion."

The Burdens of History

"To Thine Own Self"
No "single star," Rolfe argues, not even the Soviet Union's red star, can prove unwavering. He must instead use an inner compass to point toward what matters. The inner compass points toward the lessons of lived history; the self one can rely on takes shape in an engagement with its times. See the introduction to Rolfe's *Collected Poems* for a more detailed discussion of this poem.

"May 22nd 1939"
Toller: Ernst Toller (1893–1939) was an exiled German-Jewish dramatist and poet whom Rolfe met in Spain (*Lincoln Battalion,* 277–80). Radicalized by

the experience of thirteen months in the trenches at Verdun in World War I, in which he was wounded in 1916, Toller became a committed socialist and wrote expressionist plays of suffering and revolt against the imperial order. As a result of his role in strikes and antiwar agitation, he was imprisoned for a time. Toller was a leader in the short-lived Bavarian Soviet Republic of 1919, succeeding Kurt Eisner after his assassination. He also headed the Red Guard. When the revolution collapsed, he was imprisoned for five years. It was there that he wrote his most famous plays, including *Masses and Men, The Machine-Wreckers,* and *Brokenbrow.* His prison poems, first published in 1923, were translated as *The Swallow-Book* in 1924. One of his plays dramatizes the 1918 mutiny of sailors at Kiel. Exiled in 1932, his life became increasingly difficult. Despite translations of his work by Stephen Spender and W. H. Auden, he remained little-known in the English-speaking world. But it was not his career that was his main focus in those years; it was the struggle against fascism. A foe of the Nazis throughout his exile, Toller was the object of especially intense Nazi hatred. He was also deeply engaged in efforts to help the Spanish republic, and Franco's victory plunged him into despair. Toller committed suicide in New York in 1939. A fragmentary note in Rolfe's archive reads: "I never saw Toller dead. Even the photographs of his face among the flowers in his bier seemed strange. I never even remember him really as he was at the banquet. That was not the real thing either. I saw him when he was alive."

"the horizon of Nazi faces murdering Muehsam": Erich Muehsam (1878–1934) was a German-Jewish poet, dramatist, and anarchist. His work combines proletarian social critique with anarchist philosophy and expressionist technique. He published an anarchist newspaper, *Der Arme Teufel,* briefly just after the turn of the century and in 1911 founded another anarchist periodical, *Kain,* which lasted until 1919, except for several years during World War I. Muehsam helped organize a strike at the Krupp factories in Munich later in the war; he was imprisoned for his efforts. Like Toller, he was active in the overthrow of the Bavarian monarchy and a notable figure in the short-lived Bavarian Soviet Republic of April 1919. Sentenced to fifteen years in prison on its overthrow, he was released after five years. For nine years, until he was imprisoned by the Nazis in 1933, he edited *Fanal,* a monthly of anarchist philosophy. After being repeatedly tortured in several concentration camps, he was murdered by the Nazis at Oranienburg on July 9, 1934. In the light of Rolfe's own difficulties later in publishing "Elegia," it is worth noting that Muehsam published an elegy on the death of Lenin that compared him to Moses; the Party did not care for the biblical reference.

Like Rolfe, Toller and Muehsam were both secularized Jews and writer-revolutionaries.

NOTES TO THE POEMS

"In the Time of Hesitation"
The title is taken from William Vaughan Moody's turn-of-the-century poem against American imperialism in the Philippines, "An Ode in Time of Hesitation."

"At the Moment of Victory"
Les hommes de bonne volonté (Men of Goodwill): This is the overall title of a series of twenty-seven novels written by Jules Romains from 1932 to 1946. The series focuses on French history between 1908 and 1933 and emphasizes group movement and collective effort. Romains's protagonists tend to be politically committed and, at least at first, to be optimistic about their effect on history. Romains's own optimism came to an end with the rise of Nazism. Rolfe's concluding phrase, *Les hommes* sans *volonté*, is an ironic reversal of Romains's title.

"Exodus 1947"
The poem in manuscript is untitled. A page of notes preceding the poem, however, has this title. "Exodus 1947," unpublished in Rolfe's lifetime, is about holocaust survivors en route to Palestine. "Exodus 1947" was the name given to a ship that carried 4,554 Jewish refugees to Palestine in 1947. The trip was organized by the *Haganah*. Following a battle in which three Jews died, the ship was seized by the British near Haifa. Sent back to Europe, the passengers were forcibly removed from the ship by British soldiers. The ship's name and the poem's title, of course, refer not only to the biblical exodus from Egypt but also to the exodus as a figure for Jewish history.

In the absence of these notes, it might seem to some readers that it is also Rolfe's only poem on an explicitly Jewish theme. Actually, there are several other poems that make reference to Jewish history and anti-Semitism—including "Entry" and "Song (3)" from his *Collected Poems* and "Essay on Dreiser (1871–1945)," "May 22 1939," and "Now the Fog" in the present volume—but the references in most of these poems will not readily be recognized without the relevant background knowledge.

"Idiot Joe Prays in Pershing Square and
Gets Hauled in for Vagrancy"
Earlier drafts had the titles "En La Noche Oscura" and "The Prayer of Joe Blix the Anarchist."

"The Glory Set"
The stamps were given to Rolfe by Clifford Odets. The first draft of the poem began "Dear Clifford." It was titled "Lines to a Friend."

"On Rico LeBrun's *Crucifixion*"

Rico Lebrun was an artist on the Left whom Rolfe met in Los Angeles. Lebrun's series of 206 paintings and drawings on the theme of the crucifixion was exhibited at the Los Angeles County Museum from January 27 to February 28, 1951. The poem may focus partly on the large (192-by-312-inch) triptych that opened the exhibit. The exhibit catalogue was in Rolfe's library.

"Poem"

"*Consciousness,* said Don Miguel, *is a disease*": The quotation is from the first chapter of Unamuno's *The Tragic Sense of Life* (1913). Rolfe's papers include the following fragment, titled "On reading a book by M. de U.":

> Not with its sense, not with its logic,
> Nor with its sad philosophy—
> but with its dire predicament I agree.

"Night World"

Compare the very different poem with the same title in *First Love* in Rolfe's *Collected Poems.*

Summons to the Inquisition

"Now the Fog"

The reference to Juan Ponce de León and his 1513 voyage to the Americas in the third stanza will be recognizable to most readers. On the other hand, the historical reference at issue in the image of "the colorless Pale / of a stamped official registration card" in the previous stanza may be less familiar. Rolfe is suggesting that, if we go on as we are, we will soon find the United States to be as repressive and restrictive as czarist Russia was to the Jews. The Pale of Settlement was the restricted territory in czarist Russia where Jews were authorized to live. Even within the Pale, Jews were generally prohibited from living in rural areas. In the late nineteenth century and the early twentieth, Jewish villages within the Pale were subjected to the pogroms. Effectively ended by population displacements during World War I, the law establishing the Pale was overturned after the 1917 revolution.

"All Ghouls' Night"

An earlier draft is titled "Conspiracy."

"Ballad of the Noble Intentions"

This poem was written in response to hearing that his friend Clifford Odets had testified before HUAC and named names. It was first titled "Ballad of the Lost Friend." Rolfe and Odets had known one another since the 1930s.

"Political Prisoner 123456789"

Rolfe had in mind a reference to the Hollywood Ten, minus Edward Dmytryk, who, after initial resistance, turned and cooperated with HUAC. The ten "un-friendly" witnesses, all Hollywood writers or film directors, who were called to tes-tify before HUAC in Washington in October 1947 were John Howard Lawson, Dalton Trumbo, Albert Maltz, Alvah Bessie, Samuel Ornitz, Herbert Biberman, Edward Dmytryk, Adrian Scott, Ring Lardner, Jr., and Lester Cole. They stood on their First Amendment rights to freedom of speech and association in refusing to disclose their own and other people's political associations. Cited for contempt of Congress, they lost their appeals and eventually served time in federal prison. See the Introduction for further comments on the poem. For a time Rolfe's wife, Mary, was in charge of organizing efforts for the Hollywood Ten.

"A Poem to Delight My Friends
Who Laugh at Science-Fiction"

This was inspired in part by a *New York Times* story. See the Introduction.

"Are You Now or Have You Ever Been"

The poem is typed, but the title is printed somewhat roughly in holograph.

"A Letter to the Denouncers"

There are several drafts of this poem in the archive, but this is clearly the latest version.

"1949 (After Reading a News Item)"

An earlier draft has the title "1949: On Reading One News Item and Recalling Another." Pius XII became pope in 1939 and enthusiastically celebrated Franco's victory. The previous pope had also spoken out in support of Franco during the Spanish Civil War.

"June 19, 1953"

The poem is untitled. We gave it a dated title to make it consistent with the other quatrains involving a historical comparison. That the poem compares the U.S. Supreme Court's roles in the executions of Sacco and Vanzetti and the Rosenbergs is not in doubt. The date we assigned, however, may not be correct, since the court was also involved in the Rosenberg case the previous year (1952), when it refused to review it. It was on June 19, 1953, that the Supreme Court convened for a spe-cial session, returning from vacation for that purpose, in order to vacate a stay of execution that had been granted by Justice William O. Douglas. The Rosenbergs were executed that evening. The phrase "kills Jews today" seemed to argue for the 1953 date, which also assumes that Rolfe meant "twenty-five years ago" to be a rhetorical figure for the year (1927) when Sacco and Vanzetti were executed. In any case, the poem carries the same force whether it was written in response to the 1952 or 1953 decision.

Julius and Ethel Rosenberg were accused of passing data on the construction of the atomic bomb to the Soviet Union. Although no documentary evidence of espionage was presented at their 1951 trial, which occurred during the period of anticommunist hysteria in the United States, they were promptly convicted and sentenced to death. Some of the oral testimony against them has since been shown to have been fabricated. Whether they were guilty or innocent, therefore, it seems clear that some testimony was perjured and that the case against them did not meet the legal burden of proof.

"Little Ballad for Americans—1954"

Rolfe's title no doubt alludes ironically to Earl Robinson's famous 1939 patriotic cantata *Ballad for Americans,* which set to music John Latouche's 1935 poem of the same title. Rolfe and Robinson knew one another and collaborated on two projects. In the 1930s Rolfe did the words and Robinson the music for a dance for Jane Dudley, one of Martha Graham's dancers. In 1948 Rolfe wrote the verse accompaniment and Robinson wrote the music for the Joseph Strick–Irving Lerner short film *Muscle Beach.* Robinson himself was blacklisted in the 1950s. Moreover, Robinson's *Ballad for Americans* gained national fame in 1939 when it was performed on radio by Paul Robeson and then recorded and released by RCA. By the time Rolfe wrote his poem Robeson too was blacklisted in the entertainment industry, and Robeson's passport had been revoked so as to prevent him from performing abroad. Years earlier, incidentally, Rolfe was one of a group of students at the Experimental College at Wisconsin who found a place for Robeson to stay while he performed in Madison; none of the hotels would rent a room to a black man. Rolfe's poem thus resonates with intertwined personal and historical allusions; none are necessary to the poem, but they enrich its ironies and add a personal element to its composition. More broadly, the reference to Robinson's *Ballad for Americans* underlines the difference between the idealized image of America and its reality during the inquisition. *Ballad for Americans* is an inclusive, Whitmanesque celebration of all the ethnic, religious, and racial groups that make up America; during the McCarthy period the dominant culture was obsessed instead with casting people out as un-American.

UNIVERSITY OF ILLINOIS PRESS
1325 SOUTH OAK STREET
CHAMPAIGN, ILLINOIS 61820-6903
WWW.PRESS.UILLINOIS.EDU